NOW WE CAN SPEAK

A Journey through the New Nicaragua

NOW WE CAN SPEAK
A Journey through the New Nicaragua

by Frances Moore Lappé and Joseph Collins

Photographs by Peter Barnes, Susan Meiselas, Margaret Randall and Jamey Stillings

Food First Institute for Food and Development Policy
1885 Mission Street San Francisco, CA 94103-3584 USA

Library of Congress Catalog Card Number: 82-21289
ISBN: 0-935028-14-5

Printed in the United States of America

1 2 3 4 5 6 7 8 9

To order additional copies of this book, please call or write:

Institute for Food and Development Policy
1885 Mission St.
San Francisco, CA 94103 USA
(415) 864-8555

Please add 15 percent for postage and handling ($1 minimum).
Bulk discounts available.

Distributed in the United Kingdom by:

Third World Publications
151 Stratford Rd.
Birmingham B11 1RD
England

Design: Nancy Guinn
Printing: McNaughton & Gunn, Ann Arbor
Type: Aurora Type, Berkeley
Display face: Bookman Demi Italic
Text face: Bookman Light

Photographs on pages 11, 15, 23, 27, 29, 31, 33, 37, 45, 87, 105
by Peter Barnes.
Photographs on pages 7, 41, 49, 59, 63, 69, 73, 77, 81, 89, 93,
97 by Margaret Randall.
Photographs on pages viii, 6, 14, 26, 36, 48, 104 by Jamey
Stillings.
Photographs on pages 19, 53, 62, 68, 80, 96, 112 by Susan
Meiselas/Magnum.
Photograph on page vii by Nick Allen.

Library of Congress Cataloging in Publication Data

Lappé, Frances Moore.
  Now we can speak.

  Bibliography: p.
    1. Food supply—Government policy—Nicaragua.
2. Agriculture and state—Nicaragua.   3. Nicaragua—
Social conditions.   4. Nicaragua—Politics and government—
1979-   . 5. Nicaragua—Economic conditions—1979-
I. Collins, Joseph, 1945-   . II. Institute for Food and
Development Policy (San Francisco, Calif.) III. Title.
HD9014.N52L36 1982   338.1'9'7285   82-21289
ISBN 0-935028-14-5 (pbk.)

Table of Contents

Joseph Collins and Frances Moore Lappé

Acknowledgments

Thanks first to the entire staff of the Institute for Food and Development Policy, especially Nick Allen for his invaluable editing, Steve Goldfield for his help in word processing, and Nancy Guinn for her production contribution.

We are grateful to the many people in Nicaragua who gave so generously of their time to tell us their stories. We spoke with many more people than we were able to include in this book. We thank each of you.

Man practicing writing, a result of the literary crusade in Miskito, Pantipitu

Now We Can Speak

"We used to be like mute people," Jesús Lopez Garcia told us. "But now we can speak."

Jesús is a peasant woman living in the village of Santa Maria in northern Nicaragua. She is one of the dozens of people we spoke with on our visit to Nicaragua in February 1982, two and a half years after a popular uprising overthrew the brutal, 45-year-long Somoza dictatorship. We met members of newly formed farm cooperatives, marketplace vendors, the manager of Managua's biggest supermarket, the director of the agrarian reform program, American priests and nuns, leaders of the country's largest unions and many more. To each we posed similar questions: How is the revolution changing your life? What are your problems, your hopes and fears for the future? How did you come to be so involved?

They were all eager to tell us their stories. And that is what this book is about.

In August 1979, our Institute received a long distance call from Managua, Nicaragua. On the line was an official in Nicaragua's Ministry of Planning. He asked for Joe Collins. "We're putting together an advisory panel with experience in problems of agrarian reform and food policy. We think highly of your work. Would you be willing to come down for a working session to discuss Nicaragua's food and farming policies? An international church group will pay your way."

This call did not come completely out of the blue: since founding the Institute for Food and Development Policy in 1975 and publishing our book, *Food First: Beyond the Myth of Scarcity*, in 1977, we have been in contact with people all over the world working to develop more just and effective food and farming systems.

As students of the causes of and proposed remedies for world hunger for many years, the theme of our work can be summed up in one sentence: Hunger cannot be eliminated without basic political and economic changes that redistribute power over food-producing resources. So naturally we sit up and take notice when a government claims—as does the Nicaraguan government—to be making just such redistributive changes.

Indeed, we took special note of Nicaragua because, before the overthrow of the dictatorship, most Nicaraguans had been made among the poorest people in Latin America, despite the agricultural wealth of their country.

But we have learned to be leery of government claims of concern for the poor. We've documented how governments in India, Brazil, the Philippines and elsewhere, claiming to be concerned about the hungry, launch costly aid-financed programs to increase food production. But despite production successes, hunger deepens precisely because these governments repress the very movements for change which would redistribute power over basic resources and allow people to benefit from increased production. In other countries, some calling themselves socialist, the well-being of rural people has been sacrificed for rapid urban industrialization.

Will Nicaragua be different?

Of course, we can't predict the future. But many of the Nicaraguans we met stressed that their revolution is distinctly Nicaraguan. Starting from their unique past and present, they said they want to learn from the mistakes of other societies in transition, not repeat them.

Nicaragua is a country the size of Pennsylvania, located between Honduras and Costa Rica. Despite the fact that five acres of land were under cultivation for each person—twice what we have in the United States—almost 60 percent of all children under the age of four were underfed. And, by the 1970s, 60 percent of rural people had been deprived of the land they needed to feed themselves while 1.4 percent monopolized over 40 percent.

The U.S. Marines occupied Nicaragua for almost 21 straight years from 1912 to 1933, leaving only after they had installed one of the most corrupt and brutal regimes in the Americas, the Somozas, who allied themselves more closely with the U.S. government than with the Nicaraguan people. (So dominated was Nicaragua that, as late as the 1940s, its national treasury was housed in Hartford, Connecticut!)

By the mid-1970s, practically everyone in the country declared "Basta!"—we've had enough. The workers in the few cities and the farmers and landless workers in the countryside, organized by the Sandinista Front for National Liberations (FSLN), were joined by shopkeepers, businessmen, professionals—even the sons and daughters of Somocista families—

to fight the dictatorship.

Finally, on July 17, 1979, with 50,000 dead and the economy in ruins, Anastasio Somoza Debayle fled to Miami and the Sandinistas marched triumphantly into the capital city.

A Common Legacy

Although Nicaragua's revolution is uniquely Nicaraguan, it shares a legacy with most underdeveloped countries, an economic and social structure deformed by centuries of foreign domination:

—A small elite monopolizing control over economic resources, denying the majority the minimal necessities of life. Under Somoza, a mere 1,600 people controlled almost half of the agricultural land.

—Good land underused and the best land used not to grow food for Nicaraguans but luxury exports to further enrich the already wealthy. Almost 22 times more land was used to produce exports than to grow staple foods.

—An extraordinary dependence on—and therefore vulnerability to—the international market. Nicaragua's entire economy can be undermined if the price of one of its four major export products drops a few cents on the London commodity exchange.

—No experience in democratic process. Indeed, decades of iron-clad dictatorship taught Nicaraguans that to speak out is to risk your life.

—The lack of experienced leaders, administrators, technicians, and managers with which to build a new society.

In addition to this historical legacy of distorted development, the new government has had to face the massive destruction of the war. Driving into Managua from the airport, bombed-out shells of factories reminded us that Somoza had ordered the National Guard to bomb the cities, even the factories, to punish Nicaraguans for their impudence in opposing him. The final cost was 50,000 killed, 100,000 wounded and $2.8 billion in destruction and capital flight.

In his final years, Somoza also ran up a $1.6 billion debt to foreign banks and multilateral lenders, much of which went either for weapons or into his secret foreign accounts. In his final days, he looted the national treasury, leaving a pitiful $2 million. The Sandinistas thus came to power saddled with a gigantic national debt incurred in part in the dictator's attempt to destroy them.

In 1982, compounding problems of reconstruction, unprecedented floods destroyed crops, farmland, homes, roads and bridges valued at $350 million.

Nicaragua is also trapped in the economic crisis

hitting all of Central America. Prices for the region's basic exports have fallen while prices have soared for energy and manufactured goods—almost all of which it must import. In 1970, a 100-pound bag of Nicaraguan coffee bought 100 barrels of oil; today, only three. The world prices of all three of Nicaragua's most important exports—coffee, cotton, and sugar—had fallen to their lowest levels in ten years by 1982.

A Critical Openness

Through Joe's seminars after each of his visits to Nicaragua as an unpaid advisor, all of us at the Institute have been impressed by the prudent and participatory manner in which the new food and farming programs are being carried out. But we also know that Nicaragua is extremely controversial. Some Americans, forgetting their own revolution, doubt that any revolution can do more than substitute a new elite for the old. Some critics doubt whether any government in which one party has as much strength as the Sandinistas can fail to move in an authoritarian direction.

But our experience leads us to resist the temptation to pass a verdict on the new Nicaragua, just three years old. Passing a verdict would be to make Nicaragua captive to our preconceptions about revolutionary change, denying the genuine creativity of so much that seems to be happening in Nicaragua today.

Rather, we want to learn as much as possible about the process of change underway there. We want to try to see that process from the viewpoint of the Nicaraguans themselves. Of course, we will remain critical, raising questions or fears over specific issues where we feel them, not condemning or praising the entire undertaking.

To gain from this venture in critical openness, we must first answer two questions: Are we willing even to entertain the idea that there may be ways to organize economic and political life—*different* from the ones we know—that serve the material and moral needs of the majority? And is it at least possible that we, here in the United States, might be able to learn from these different approaches?

Obviously, we have answered these questions in the affirmative. We hope that in picking up this book you feel a similar desire to be both open and critical.

It is in this spirit that we would like to introduce you to the people we met during our visit. Wanting you to understand Nicaraguans as they see themselves, we have tried to let them speak for themselves.

We Are Landing

Saturday night, February 6, 1982. We are landing. From the window we can see the lights of the city below. The 1972 earthquake that demolished the center of Managua, the capital of Nicaragua, encouraged its spread, so that from the night sky it looks like a mini-Los Angeles.

Our traveling party consists of the two of us, Joe and Frances, plus Peter Barnes, president of a cooperative solar installation business in San Francisco and a former journalist whose work includes *The People's Land: A Reader on Land Reform in America.*

During much of our journey, Father Peter Marchetti, an American Jesuit working with the Nicaragua Ministry of Agriculture and a friend of Joe for many years, was our knowledgeable guide. He completed his doctoral work in sociology at Yale by studying the agrarian reform in Allende's Chile and has since worked in several other Latin American countries.

Coffee bags at coffee drying area near Matagalpa

Jamey Stillings

Caliche

Our Journey

Monday afternoon, still jet-lagged but eager to get going, we were driven by Peter Marchetti south from Managua. Our destination was a local headquarters of the Sandinista Front in the Masaya region.

"Only one change really counts"

We had read that the Sandinista leadership is young but we still weren't prepared when Caliche Borrios came out to greet us. He is 20—just barely. Slender and softspoken, he seemed almost shy. His office is in a drab, sparsely furnished house abandoned by a fleeing ally of the ousted dictator.

Caliche is not employed by the government but by the Sandinista Front to work directly with the poor-est peasants and landless people in the area around Ticuantepe. There he helps them develop programs and pressure the government for policies that will benefit them.

We first asked about his life.

"My father—he's dead now—was a fairly modern-ized rancher and I've always loved living in the countryside. I didn't begin to understand what was happening in our country until I was a teenager. As a student at the Jesuit high school, with five of my schoolmates I joined a youth group led by a priest. The heart of our work was living with poor people here in this zone. We studied and tried to apply the teaching techniques of Paulo Freire. We got involved in everything—in sports, in the concerns of the youth and the health problems. But all our work had to be clandestine because of the National Guard."

From Caliche's office we drove out the dirt roads to see the mountainous terrain onto which poor farmers had been pushed by the big cotton growers who progressively had taken over the good flat valley lands. We took advantage of the time to press Caliche on a question that especially intrigued us: what makes it possible for people to make such changes in their lives?

He was silent for a moment. Then he answered: "There is only one change that really counts. As long as poor people see themselves as *pobreterria* there is no hope for change. That is what has to change."

What does *pobreterria* mean? There's no exact translation, but it would be the equivalent of poor people here calling themselves good-for-nothings—the scum of the earth, the bottom of the barrel.

"As long as people are ashamed and blame them-selves for their poverty, things cannot change. All of our work is to change that view of themselves."

But how?

"We try to take people through three steps. First, they must see the real injustices that keep them poor. It's nothing for *them* to be ashamed of. Second they must understand *how* this came to be—that it wasn't always this way and doesn't have to always be. Third, we show that their situation is national—that they are not alone. Theirs are the problems of the majority of our people."

By then Peter Marchetti had stopped our jeep so that we could take a picture of a new clinic built by the people in the area. A poor peasant walking by paused to offer us some rolls. He and Caliche joked like old friends.

"You don't just shout slogans . . . "

As we continued our drive, Caliche talked about his own views of the direction the Sandinista Front should now take.

"You don't just shout slogans at people," he told us. "What we must do is bring the content of political speeches into people's lives. They must see that something is changing in their lives—new popularly controlled stores, new roofs, new schools, many people getting land for the first time. Otherwise they'll just see the speeches of our national leaders as propaganda.

"Before, during the armed struggle against Somoza, it was easier to motivate people. We could inspire people to get involved by telling them about those who had gone to fight, who were risking their lives. But it's different now. We can point to our martyrs, but it is less directly personal.

"Our problem is that we had achieved a high enough level of consciousness to win the war against Somoza but not to deal with our real problems now. We just can't expect that the level of consciousness necessary to win the war will carry us now. So I think we Sandinistas have to come back to the people. There was a real democratization going on in our country during the years of organizing before we overthrew the dictatorship. That organizing works, especially when there are real material gains, when people can see the changes. And you can even do without material gains so long as there is unity and identification with the people."

"They smell the moist earth"

The sun was going down. It was time to take Caliche back to his office. He was eager to finish a position paper—his view of what should be done about the agrarian problems in the area. The paper would be presented to his higher-ups in the Front. His proposals capture the many contradictions the Sandinistas have to confront in making policies that benefit the poor while not alienating wealthy producers or sacrificing desperately needed foreign exchange.

"People need land: that's a big problem in this area, maybe our biggest," Caliche told us. "But the only good land belongs to the big cotton growers who moved into this area in the fifties and pushed the peasants up into the hills. The agrarian reform law says we can't take any of that land back for the peasants."

Caliche was referring to the August 1981 law which stipulates that land cannot be confiscated and redistributed to the landless unless its owner does not use it productively.

"Even if the peasants were given enough land to feed themselves," he told us, "they would still be willing to work on the plantations."

Caliche was responding to a big concern of the government: if seasonal farmworkers who have traditionally harvested the export crops get their own land, will they still be willing to work for wages on the export estates? If not, the country's already desperate foreign exchange situation could suffer.

"Are we going to respond to the people's demand for land? That's the question. The government should declare this area a special case and expropriate some of the land from the largest estates—even if the owners are cultivating it—and give it back to the poorest peasants. There have to be exceptions. Otherwise the peasants here are just going to seize the land themselves. And that will be much worse."

It had rained lightly that day, almost unheard of for this time of year.

"The rain will make it more difficult to stop people from taking the land. Now the peasants smell the moist earth. They begin to think of planting corn and beans. And when the peasants think of planting, they think of getting land."

By then we had returned to Caliche's office. Arriving at the same time was Arturo, a young man whose dimpled smile made him immediately likeable. As a teenager, Arturo had been part of the same youth group at the Jesuit high school that Caliche had told us about. They were close friends and now Arturo was working for the division of the agricultural ministry responsible for planning for small farmers.

Caliche and Arturo agreed that, together with the local campesinos, they should convince the Sandinista Front and the government to make an exception here and give some land to the peasants. As Caliche went inside to draft his position paper, maybe with Arturo's coaching, we headed back to Managua.

As we drove, we thought of our typical images of "party militants." Caliche's soft-spoken, easygoing manner just didn't fit at all. Another stereotype of revolutionary governments is that decisions get made from the top down. Yet we learned that one of the government's biggest headaches was trying to resist the demands of the peasants in order not to threaten the well-off landowners.

(Caliche's arguments for the land must have been convincing because a few months later, Joe found Caliche busy working with campesinos moving them onto new lands.)

"They look at you funny"

Vendor in Managua's Mercado oriental

The next morning before our first scheduled interview, we strolled through Managua's biggest market—the Mercado Oriental, or Eastern Market. It is huge, covering many city blocks. There you can buy anything from fruit, to plastic bowls, to notebooks, to a hot meal.

Within minutes, a woman vendor caught our eyes.

"Are you North Americans?" she asked. "What are you doing here? The government says that North Americans are our enemies, so why do they let you come here?"

We explained that the government didn't consider the *people* of North America to be the enemy—only the U.S. government. But it was clear that the woman wanted to talk with us, so we asked her what she thought of the Sandinista government.

"Oh, it's repressive," she told us, frowning and

shaking her hand in the air.

How? How is it repressive? we asked.

"All I want to do is work. I just want to be left alone to do my work. I work hard. But they want you to come to meetings—to the CDS [neighborhood group] meetings—and they expected everybody to be in literacy campaign. Come on, it's not possible to learn to read and write in a few months. It's just not possible, you know that. And I'm too tired to learn. I work hard.

"If you don't go to the meetings, people look at you funny," she charged, putting a finger up to her right eye.

Has anyone done anything to you for not coming to the meetings?

"No, but they look at you funny. And those meetings don't do any good. What do they accomplish?"

You don't think the CDS groups have done anything to help the market?

"No, nothing." She paused for a moment. "Well, it did start a day care center for the children of parents working here. But another thing," she went on. "If you don't join the militia, you can't get a job."

When we asked whether she actually knew anyone who had been denied a job because of not being in the militia, she said "no."

Well, since you don't like the Sandinista government, would you prefer a return to a Somoza-type government and the National Guard?

"Oh, my God, no!" Her hands flew up in the air. "God hold my tongue," she exclaimed. "Even God doesn't love those people!"

Our conversation with the market vendor made us begin to realize that no matter how beneficial the programs pushed by the new government, there are those in *any* society who just want to be left alone, and who resent any pressure on them to get involved. An important test for Nicaragua, and for all poor societies which must by necessity depend on their people's initiative, will be just how they end up dealing with the just-leave-me-alone-ers.

We were late for our next appointment, but luckily we found a taxi. Getting in we noticed the taxi's radio was tuned to a local AM station rebroadcasting the news in Spanish from the Voice of America.

We hadn't ridden far when the driver, apparently sensing that we were North Americans, broke into our conversation. "There's no freedom here," he volunteered.

We asked him what made him say that.

"The Sandinista traffic police give out tickets for speeding and running red lights. And there's no way you can get out of them. Before you never got fined; you could always get by with a little bribe."

We told him there might be fewer accidents with good police enforcement of traffic rules. Somewhat to our amazement, he readily agreed:

"Yes. You know, I had a friend, also a taxi driver, who once ran a red light and killed a pedestrian. The next day the dead man's friends swore revenge and set out to kill my friend. Things got so dangerous for him that he fled the country. Now he's living in California."

Man shoveling dry coffee, at La Estrella, a state-owned coffee farm near Matagalpa

Jamey Stillings

Visiting a State Coffee Farm

We're on our way again, this time north to visit a state coffee farm, La Unidad, with Father Peter Marchetti. About 20 percent of the agricultural land in Nicaragua was now in state farms, created from the properties abandoned by Somoza and his close associates, such as the officers of the National Guard.

State farms are one of the most controversial issues of noncapitalist development. For some, they are the epitome of everything that is wrong with socialism. They are bureaucratic, run top-down, and frightfully inefficient. Others see state farms as the highest form of agriculture because, being publicly controlled, they can benefit the entire society instead of just making a handful wealthy.

La Unidad, a state coffee farm near Esteli

Just where did the Sandinista leadership stand? Were they planning to expand state control over agriculture?

Peter said "no."

Did the Sandinistas start out enamored of the state farm model?

"Of course," Peter told us, "is the Pope Catholic? But reality soon muddied their idealized vision of state farms as the sole answer. Campesino cooperatives in the cotton areas are out-producing the state farms. Now they're trying to create a balanced mix with support for the state farms, the campesino cooperatives, and the private farms, large and small.

"Now the ministry is strictly judging each state farm on its efficiency as well as its social role. Those that can't prove themselves profitable (and are not part of a special development project) are being turned over to cooperatives and, in some cases, to family farmers."

Now we are approaching Esteli. During the insurrection, Somoza ordered the bombing of the hospital here and even prevented the Red Cross from entering.

In the war, Estelí lost almost one-quarter of its people. The bombed-out buildings were still evident, and bullet holes marked the entry way wall as we entered the government agricultural offices.

At the office we pick up the head of the state coffee farms in the area. A serious man in his forties, wearing slightly tinted glasses and blue jeans, he explained that he was from Honduras but had lived in Nicaragua sixteen years. Later he told us that he owned his own coffee estate, which he oversaw on weekends. (The Sandinistas certainly aren't rigid ideologues, we thought, if they allow a capitalist producer to hold a position of such authority.) As we drove out to the state farm, we asked why he had started working for the state.

"The revolution needs technicians," was his first answer. But then he added, "Before, I worked only with my relatives. And that can have its problems. I really like working for the state."

We'd never thought about government employment as a way to escape uncomfortable family ties! We asked: Do you feel pushed to become more political now that you are working for the government?

"No, I don't feel pushed but it's happening. Before there were many things I didn't take into account. Really, I only thought about my salary. Of course, I'm still concerned about my salary! But I can also see the needs of the workers and all the problems we have to overcome."

As we drove from his office to the state coffee farm—miles away—we were climbing. The vegetation became more lush. The cooler, moister climate was ideal for coffee, we were told.

The farm looked dreary and run down, not posh as you might expect an estate previously owned by an ally of Somoza. Then we were reminded that the wealthy owners rarely live at the estates. The former owner of this farm owned six others but lived in the capital. Now he's in Honduras, plotting to overthrow the Sandinista government.

As the farm's managers told us their stories, we began to appreciate how difficult it is to judge the efficiency of a state farm, even after two and a half years. There are more workers now but output is about the same. "Doesn't that mean a fall in productivity?" we asked.

"No, you don't understand. We're investing in improvements. It takes a lot of workers to do that. You can't expect to see more coffee yet. It takes three years for a coffee tree to mature."

The previous owner had let the estate run down. Now it would take years of special attention to plant new varieties and to adjust planting densities, shade, and fertilizer applications in order to reach the goal of almost tripling production per acre.

"Now there is an objective standard"

Like the state farm itself, the role of the labor union in a socialist or mixed economy is controversial. Is a union simply a tool for government control of the workers? Or can it be a powerful representative of workers' interests and vehicle for worker participation in management impossible under capitalism?

For Nicaragua, as in probably most third world countries, these questions aren't entirely applicable, Peter told us. Most workers in Nicaragua, if literate at all, are barely able to read and write; their first demand is not to participate in "management." On state farms the role of the "union"—the Association of Rural Workers—seems to be more to protect the workers from arbitrary treatment by the farm's managers.

"If I just fired someone unilaterally, the association could take it to the Ministry of Labor. I need the agreement of the association to fire," an administrator told us.

No doubt the administrators also see the association as a help in their efforts to increase production.

"The association can help make workers aware of the importance of productivity and can oversee the quality of work." an administrator told us.

While not really involved in management, the association appeared to have some role in planning the work schedule.

"The association meeting is where the monthly work plan is presented and discussed. The workers tell us what they think. They might say, 'No, that's impossible, we can't do that much.' Or they might say, 'we can do more than that; let's try' and we would have to change our plans."

We tried to get a sense of what has changed in the

lives of the workers since the farm went from private to state ownership. Clearly there has been no dramatic change. But, as one manager put it, "At least now there is a clear, objective standard set by the state as to salary, food and working conditions. If the administration of the farm doesn't meet these standards, the workers can go over its head to the Ministry."

Before, under Somoza, enforcement of even the minimum wage law was so rare that many workers didn't even know a minimum wage law was on the books. As we left La Unidad and headed further north toward the the Honduran border, we checked out our impressions with Peter. Honestly, would the workers really use their power to go over the heads of their bosses? We were astonished when Peter told us that he knew of twenty cases where pressure from the workers had ended up actually removing the farm administrators.

The workers can see the incompetence of an administrator better than someone sitting in the capital, Peter explained. On the large private farms and ranches, the workers are also on the lookout for "decapitalization" by owners. Some large landowners have refused to invest in their farms, letting them run down, selling off their cattle and equipment, and moving their assets out of the country to bank accounts in Miami or Panama. From mid-1980 to mid-1981, "de-capitalization" drained an estimated $500 million from the hard-pressed Nicaraguan economy. Under the Agrarian Reform Law, published in August 1981, workers' denunciations have led to expropriation of farms whose owners were deliberately letting them run down.

Bumping along in the jeep, Peter tried to calculate the workers' present wages and benefits, compared to what they were under Somoza. He concluded that they had risen 30 percent in real terms, which seemed to surprise him. Most of that increase has come in the form of more expensive food—some meat and eggs each week, which workers never before enjoyed. (Three meals a day are free; together with other fringe benefits they are worth almost half as much as the average daily cash wages.)

ENABAS storefront in countryside near Esteli

North to Santa Maria

At the regional office for agriculture and agrarian reform, we added to our party Father Antonio Cabellas, a Spanish-born Jesuit, and his sister, visiting from Spain. Having Antonio with us turned out to be an enormous asset. He knew the whole area intimately; and as was clear with each new person we met, he was respected and loved by the people there.

The farther north we drove, the bumpier and more winding the road. But as we approached Santa Maria we were rewarded by striking vistas of the valleys below. As we drove, Antonio talked about the attacks from across the border by members of Somoza's hated National Guard.

"It started about 18 months ago. The ex-Guardsmen are camped across the border. Every few weeks they come in, ambushing people and taking over villages—just long enough to terrorize people and shout anti-communist speeches. I can think of 18 incidents, although there could have been more. Less than a week ago, a village just six miles from Santa Maria was attacked and several people killed. Some 200 have been assassinated in this way, including teachers, health workers, campesino organizers, campesinos in the militia, and even small children.

We wondered why we weren't more frightened. We also wondered why Peter had suggested we come here! Peter explained that precisely because the attack had just happened last week, there was little danger of another so soon. Hmm. Also, he said we couldn't appreciate the changes underway in Nicaragua unless we visited the remote areas.

... *to fight food price speculation*

Our first stop, on the outskirts of the village of Santa Maria was an outlet of ENABAS, the government agency responsible for distributing some of the country's basic foods at controlled prices. The objective was to distribute enough of each basic food at controlled prices to hold the lid on the prices of the rest sold by private merchants.

A one-room adobe building, with a pig pen on one side and mounds of corn on the other, it certainly didn't look like a store of any kind. There was no ENABAS sign outside. Later the manager told us that he asked ENABAS not to place an identifying sign on the building. He feared that he would be singled out for attack by the counter-revolutionaries coming in from Honduras.

We gathered in the small, unlit room, which looked more like a poorly stocked warehouse than a store. On the floor were bags of beans, rice, corn and sugar. On the shelves were oil, basic medicines like cough syrup, soap, crackers and some envelopes of "Maggi" soup mix.

Prices were our first question. How did they compare with the private mom-and-pop type stores in Santa Maria? Sugar, we learned, sold for 2.50 cordobas elsewhere, but for only 2.00 here. (2.50 cordobas was the equivalent of 25 cents at the official rate of 10 cordobas to the U.S. dollar. However, comparisons are misleading. A farmworker picking cotton earns 50 cordobas a day.) Salt, oil, and other basic foods were comparably cheaper in the ENABAS outlet. Yet out of a total population of 5,500 in the area, only about 950 buy sugar here. Why didn't more people shop here? we wondered.

"We don't have everything a family needs," the ENABAS manager explained. So, coming here means an extra shopping trip. You still have to go to the private store. That means a good walk, and the distances here are great."

Second, at the mom-and-pop store, people are pressured by the proprietor they may have known all their lives. The outlet manager explained to us, "People just feel embarrassed to go into the private stores and buy only the extras and then come here for the basics. And some of the private storeowners refuse to sell to people unless they buy everything from him."

Both explanations made sense. But, we were told, it may also be a question of habit. The routine of daily shopping is so much a part of people's lives that making a change is difficult.

Store front outlets like this one are only one of the ways that the government, through ENABAS, seeks to ensure affordable, stable prices for basic foods. Rather than create a lot of government-owned stores, ENABAS, as a wholesaler, uses small private retailers as outlets. ENABAS offers mom-and-pop stores—selected by the neighborhood because they are trusted—the basic items at wholesale prices that allow for a sufficient profit when resold at the official retail prices. As in many other aspects of government programs, there seemed to be a lot of flexibility.

We asked the ENABAS outlet manager why the food there hadn't been distributed through the private stores.

"Because the owners don't like the conditions that ENABAS sets. They wouldn't be content with the profits. They want to charge whatever they can get."

Superficially it would appear that the government efforts to get basic food to the poor of the Santa Maria area are falling short—just another good idea that got bogged down when it met the real life habits of people. But to dismiss it like this is too easy. For however slight the dent this outlet makes in the market, its manager is convinced that it does help keep prices down.

"If this store closed," he told us, "prices in the private stores would shoot up." Father Antonio, who has lived in the area, agreed.

Store Front Education

We hopped back in the jeep and went on into the village of Santa Maria, stopping only to snap a picture of a little boy standing in front of a handsome new elementary school, one of the three new ones we spotted that day.

In the village three young women greeted us in the plain storefront office of an adult education center, stacked high with books and notebooks. Their shyness could not hide their pride in what they were doing. Nicaragua's 1980 literacy campaign reduced illiteracy from 50 to almost 13 percent. Now, the adult education centers build on this success, giving newly literate adults the equivalent of an elementary education while teaching skills immediately useful in their daily lives.

We invited them to tell us about the center.

"There are two centers in Santa Maria, 23 in the whole municipality. In our area, 800 people entered the literacy program and more than half finished. We now have 331 in our center. Some have just learned to read and write; others knew how but never had had any real schooling."

Why did people drop out? And how do you try to motivate people to take advantage of this program?

"Some people just don't want to participate. Others really try hard but just can't. They say they just can't remember things. And some just can't see and they don't have enough money for glasses.

"We try to get people interested by telling them that if they can't read, they won't know what's going on. They won't be able to participate fully in all the changes. And we tell them that we'll give them lots of free materials to help them—books, pencils and paper."

Classes are held twelve hours per week, we were told. We found it astonishing that so many poor peasants, whose lives are already physically exhausting, would voluntarily add twelve hours of mentally exhausting work to their week.

The teachers, called "coordinators," don't really get a salary, just a token stipend. In education, as in health and so many other areas, the Nicaraguans have to rely on voluntary effort. These young women were examples of the remarkable willingness of people to join in.

The government estimates that at least 40 percent of the entire population of Nicaragua is involved in some form of organized education. Just another way in which "Nicaragua is a school."

"We used to be like mutes..."

From the adult education center, Antonio directed us to the home of Jesús Lopez Garcia, a tiny, wiry woman probably in her mid-forties. It was nearly 3 p.m. and we'd had no lunch. Jesús insisted that she cook us a meal and sent the littlest child off to get some eggs. Jesús immediately put us all at ease. Her obvious affection for Padre Antonio no doubt made it easier for her to relax, even with us North Americans draped with cameras and trying to scribble down all she said.

While she and one daughter cooked, a teenage daughter took us all on a tour. First, across the hillside from their two-room house, we saw a spanking new school building. On the crest of the opposite hill we could make out a military post. Remember, we were only six miles from the Honduran border and ex-National Guardsmen had more than once invaded and attacked Santa Maria.

Down the path from the house, we passed a new well which, we were told, was bringing the neighborhood safe water for the first time. Next, we saw where at least part of our lunch was coming from—a new egg cooperative, a sturdy looking chicken coop housing several dozen chickens. We ended our tour at the new handicraft cooperative of which one of the daughters is a member. Colorful straw mats and straw cheese making strainers adorned the walls.

The young women explained that they hoped to find a way to market these handmade items in the bigger towns. We were struck as we have been so often in traveling in the third world, how even the under-development of transportation can pose an obstacle. In other words, organizing the crafts cooperative seemed relatively easy compared to the task of devising effective marketing, the next problem they had to tackle.

Our stomachs really growling by now, we returned to Jesús' home eager to eat. From atop a big earthen stove in the corner of one of her two rooms, Jesús served each of us beans, rice, a thick corn tortilla and a mound of scrambled eggs. We couldn't remember a tastier meal.

As we ate, we asked Jesús if we might ask some questions about her life. She pulled up a chair next to us, while the rest of her family stood watching, obviously proud of their outspoken mother.

Our first question was simple: How has the revolution changed your life?

"In every way.

"You saw our new well, the school, the egg and crafts cooperatives. And the village also has a new corn mill. But it's more than these things. It's very different now. Before, a lot of people were hungry. Now if you harvest your corn and beans, you can eat. Before, peo-

Jesús Lopez Garcia and her family

ple were so in debt they had to sell the food they grew. They had to mortgage their crop. Now people can get credit from the government. Now people can eat three times a day.

"And there are more jobs. Before so many people had to leave here to go to the coffee harvests. Now there are jobs nearby in reforestation (a government program) and women and children can work, too." (A few weeks later, ex-Guardsmen raided the area and burned the newly planted saplings, we learned.)

Jesús described the work of the neighborhood organizations and the municipal junta, which the Sandinistas have been setting up throughout the country. We were particularly interested in the role of the junta, or committee, something close to our town council. Peter had told us that he considered the popularly elected juntas one of the most significant aspects of the democracy the Sandinista leadership is trying to build.

"Before we used to be like mute people," Jesús told us. "But now we can speak. We elected a junta of two men and one woman. The junta helped us get the technical assistance we needed from the ministry in Managua to put in our well and it helped organize the egg cooperative."

How long do the junta members serve?

"Until we come up with a project that they just don't know enough about and then we elect somebody else."

Have you replaced anyone yet?

"Oh, yes, one just didn't work. When he came to meetings, he didn't have the information he was supposed to have. So we called a meeting to discuss the problem. We told him our complaints. And he resigned."

Before the revolution were there many supporters of Somoza here? What did people think of the Sandinistas?

"Oh, there were a lot of disagreements. Yes, there were many here who supported Somoza. You have to remember that there wasn't much fighting here. The National Guard didn't attack us like in the big cities. The Guard was king here. "

Jesús hesitated.

"The truth is, I have to say it, the majority of people here supported the Guard against the Sandinistas. For one thing, few believed the dictator could be overthrown, and everyone knew and feared his vengeance. But people have changed."

Why?

"They learned that all those things the Somoza radio said about the Sandinistas were lies. They can see the projects, the advances we've made. It's as if they had a blindness. And then the scales fell from their eyes."

By then it was almost dusk and we were anxious to

get on the road before dark. But we wanted to hear more. We learned that Jesús had also been elected to head the local women's organization, now with 36 members. Their next big project, she told us, would be to try to deal with alcoholism, a chronic problem in Santa Maria.

"We're going to have a big meeting to talk about ways to reduce the drinking problem," she said. "The junta is helping to organize it, too. And the military is behind it."

Jesús' words had been so strong and clear and the energy emanating from her tiny body seemed boundless. As she began to tell us of this next big project, we found ourselves believing that, of course, they could do it.

By the time we had all climbed into the jeep again, the day was almost gone. This meant driving back on the rough and winding road at night. With the reports of the ambushes by the ex-Guardsmen fresh in our minds, we drove fast. . .

At about 8:00 we arrived at the cathedral in Ocatal, where we were to spend the night. Another Spanish priest welcomed us and seemed to consider our spending the night on the rectory floor just the usual.

Practicing writing exercises from school, farm cooperatives near Esteli

"Now we meet as brothers"

The next morning we drove back into Estelí to pick up a government agrarian reform official who was to take us out to the new farm Noél Gámez cooperative. Alvaro Reyes is second in command in this region for the Ministry of Agriculture. Just under 30, he wore blue jeans and a short-sleeved yellow shirt; his manner was straightforward, friendly, unassuming.

As we drove to the cooperative, we asked how the agrarian reform law was being implemented. The law specifies that if land is abandoned or left idle for more than two years, or is grossly underused, it can be taken over by the government (with a variety of possible forms of compensation to the owner) and redistributed to small farmers or landless farm laborers, either

Alvaro Reyes (right) with member of Noél Gámez cooperative

as individuals or in cooperatives. This sounded reasonable and fair but we wondered just how it could be carried out. Who would decide what land was not being used productively?

"Each region is now setting up an agrarian reform council to weigh the evidence and make these decisions," Alvaro told us. "The councils are made up of representatives from the ministries of agriculture and planning, from the farmworkers organization and from the organization of small farmers, plus a legal advisor. Owners can appeal to an unfavorable decision to an agrarian reform tribunal."

Approaching the cooperative, Alvaro pointed out a grave marker.

"That is where Noél Gámez, a martyr, is buried. He was a friend of these people. He stood right there firing at the Guard, holding them off while the others escaped."

Everywhere throughout our trip we saw Nicaraguans paying tribute—small monuments, prominent gravestones, posters—to those who had died in the war. It was as if they used these reminders of their lost loved ones to help maintain their determination.

As we drove up to the farmhouse, Alvaro explained some of the history of this cooperative. The land had been owned by a Somocista, a minister in the Somoza dictatorship who died just before the "triumph." His wife and some of his children had fled to the United States, abandoning the land.

"After they fled, 21 workers—most of whom had worked on this very estate most of their lives—took it over, running it as a cooperative. That was in 1979. But the wife demanded it back. So the workers took the problem to the Association of Rural Workers (ATC) for help.

"Even though the government policy has always been against such takeovers, the association backed the workers. They thought the government should make an exception because these workers were so poor—they had no other way to feed their families. A legal battle went on for two years. It went all the way to the Supreme Court.

"The association's argument was that since the workers had already planted the land, they should be allowed to rent it. The workers accepted this. They wanted the land *any* way they could get it. But the owner—the wife now in the States—wouldn't accept a rent arrangement."

But hadn't all land abandoned by Somocistas been claimed by the government?

"Well, if the husband had lived, it would have been," Alvaro explained. "But remember he died before the triumph. So at the time of the triumph, his wife owned the land. Even though *he* was considered a

Somocista, that didn't make her one."

We were impressed that the Nicaraguans made this distinction between the responsibility of the husband and the wife. What finally happened with the land, we asked.

"The cooperative is about to get title. They've won. The agrarian reform law passed last August resolved it all. It specified that the title to land which had already been taken over by the landless and was being worked productively would go to them. So, on February 28, they'll get title and that will be the end of it."

Will the owner get paid?

"Yes, in bonds, but I can't tell you how much. The issue is still under debate in the Council of State." (See page 63 to learn more about the Council of State.)

Alvaro introduced us to some of the cooperative members. They received Alvaro like an old buddy, hardly our stereotype of the rapport between a bureaucrat and his clients! We spread out, talking to various co-op members and admiring the irrigated fields of potatoes, beans and cabbage.

"They kept their word."

The first to greet us was a man of 45, Juan Ramon Briñones Sevilla. His hat and clothes tattered, his skin showing the years of field work in the hot sun, we were moved by how much he wanted to talk with us.

Juan Ramon Briñones Sevilla

"Before the revolution, I never had spoken to a foreigner," he explained. "I had never even spoken to anyone even from Esteli. I was embarrassed. Peasants were always embarrassed even when speaking with someone from town. Now look at me. For me, this change has been an incredible thing. It's come late in my life, but I don't feel bad that it's come so late."

Juan told us that he had been born in the area.

"We were very poor. We never had any land of our own. They wouldn't even let us sharecrop this land. They only hired wage labor.

"I have ten children. They're all alive. It is very hard to have ten children and have none of them die. Now that I have land, I want to help them. They're all in school."

How did you get involved in the revolution?

"For eight years I worked with the Front (the Sandinista Front for National Liberation) but I didn't really understand. I didn't have any political or military understanding of what they were trying to do."

Why did you help then? Why did you follow blindly?

"Because they treated us well. They respected us. They gave their word and they kept it. They said they would be with us . . . stay with us . . . die with us. They kept their word.

"Someone who is prepared, who is educated—what is going on in his head may be different from what is going on in my head. We understand it all very differently. But that doesn't mean we still can't help each other.

"I helped them with food. I helped them move from one area to another." Pointing to the hills to the north, Juan continued, "We knew the terrain. They didn't. We helped them get to Honduras to get arms. For over ten years Sandinistas lived in my mother's house, secretly.

"But I've stopped working in a military way. The revolution needs me here. I can grow corn and beans. My idea is to do what I can do best—*en toda mi capacidad.* It is not for me to be running around from office to office and driving in cars. We have to grow food so the country doesn't perish."

"They said we couldn't make it . . . "

The cooperative is thinking about adding three more members—all people they know well. The cooperative is managed by a board of five elected members.

Would you consider hiring people to work for the cooperative, people who aren't members, we asked one of the members.

At that point we must have looked at Alvaro, imagining that there may be a government policy on whether cooperatives can hire labor. Alvaro seemed to have read our minds because he started laughing.

"Oh no, it's up to them," he said. "The government doesn't get involved. The cooperative must decide."

For us, this was yet another example of the lack of

ideological rigidity of the Nicaraguans.

The cooperative members then explained to us why they wouldn't be interested in hiring laborers. "It just wouldn't work. We couldn't pay enough for someone to support a family. It's much better that they become a member and share responsibility for production."

Do others want to join?

"Oh, lots of people come here. They are hungry. They want to join but they don't understand what's involved. We have to explain. We have 300,000 cordobas invested here. People have to be very serious."

By this time, we had all gathered in the field. We were introduced to a younger man, Mercedes Arce Torruño.

"I grew up here," he told us." I worked here, on this land, since I was eight years old. They used to pay me only 2 to 3 cordobas a day.

"They said we couldn't make it. The rich people said we didn't have enough knowledge. They said we'd never be able to work together. But we've done it! We've shown them that what they said about us were lies. We've shown we can produce with the help of the government."

The government has lent the cooperative all it needed for capital investment—about 300,000 cordobas. Even after the first year's production, the cooperative had a net income of approximately this amount.

Mercedes Arce Torruño

By its seventh year, it's projecting a net income of over 500,000 cordobas.

Some people in our country say that Nicaragua is "repressive." How would you respond?

"The industrialist who has lived off the blood of the people—he might feel repressed," Mercedes said. "But we are peasants. We are the people who were exploited. None of us are going to be against this revolution. Who could have imagined that someone like me could go to see the ceremony in Wiwili where other peasants got titles to land? Who would ever have believed it?"

In the United States, we're told that because your government isn't holding national elections until 1985, it is totalitarian. With no elections, there is no liberty. What do you think?

"When we started working with this revolutionary process, we were working for the poor of the country. We weren't thinking about political parties. When people start thinking about political parties, they start looking out for their own interests.

"Under Somoza we had elections, but what would happen? Only a certain group of rich people or their employees would be elected. It was a rotation of rich people in offices of power. What kind of election is that?

"Yes, elections could be a good thing. What's most important is that we know what the election process is about so it's for our benefit. The peasants and the workers in the cities would be for the elections as long as we understand they are for us. But if someone is going to come in and use the electoral process to get things moving against us, we are not going to permit it.

"I'm not against rich people—as long as they'll align themselves with our process. Take the big land-owner over there," Mercedes said, gesturing toward a nearby estate. "He has 7,000 manzanas (about 12,000 acres). Yet there are thousands of us living without any land. He doesn't have a right to all that land. If he's going to be with us, he'll have to give up some of that land. Not all of it, he can keep some for himself. Or," added Mercedes with a smile, "he can come work with us in the cooperative.

"But it doesn't look like the rich people are aligning themselves with our process. They are trying to sell all their assets and then leave. Take this guy—he's trying to sell all the timber on his property. And his cattle, he's selling that off too. Who knows, he might even get down to selling the rocks on his property!"

Everyone laughed.

"Our biggest problem is the United States taking action against us," Mercedes continued. "When the U.S. cut off wheat, a lot of small bakers here were faced with having to go out of business. It was terrible. And what if they blockade us? What if they cut off our petroleum? Even that is not going to stop us. If we have to go back to mules and oxen, we'll do it. If we have to carry bundles on our backs into the city, we'll do it. It will hurt but we'll do it."

We got up to leave. They all rose and Mercedes looked at us very seriously.

"Americans used to come here to take things away from us. Not now. Now we will shake hands. We will shake hands with you as brothers."

A Flexible Policy

As we left, we talked about cooperatives with Alvaro. We had assumed that cooperatives were being advocated by the idealistic, educated leadership, not the rural poor themselves. So much literature on third world development repeats the theme that what peasants want are their own individual plots. But what we began to see, and what the Nicaraguan leadership appears to appreciate, is that not all of the ordinary people in the countryside want the same thing.

"Of the original 21 members of the Noél Gámez cooperative we just visited, eight left. They thought it was too risky, too much work," Alvaro told us. "Some who left are doing well elsewhere. Some got jobs in the city. But now they're beginning to see how well cooperatives can do. They see all the credit the government is

Alvaro with members of Noél Gámez cooperative

giving the cooperatives to develop irrigation and other things to help them produce more than they could as individuals. Some of them now wish they'd stayed.

"Sure, cooperatives aren't easy to make work. Record keeping is one of the keys. The cooperative has to keep track of who is present, how many days each person works. So PROCAMPO (an arm of the agricultural ministry that offers technical assistance to small farmers) sent someone out to train a bookkeeper.

"In this area we're going to turn 28 state farms into cooperatives over the next year. It's just not profitable to run them as state farms. Some are in remote areas and the administrative overhead is just too high."

As Alvaro talked we were struck again at the flexibility and pragmatism of the Nicaraguan leadership— by their view that cooperatives are right for some people, but not for all; that state farms can make sense, but not in every case they've tried.

"I was very afraid..."

While we still had a few minutes with Alvaro, we were eager to know how he came to be an official of the agrarian reform here. What path had he taken?

"I was born in 1952. My father owns 1,000 manzanas (1,700 acres). He's against the revolution. He studied in the United States and thinks that the U.S.A. is the savior of the world.

"In high school I was in a group for Christian reflection led by Jesuit priests. That's where it began. We met to discuss the terrible poverty in Nicaragua and our responsibility as Christians.

"I entered the university in 1970 and joined the student movement. But I didn't know it was linked to the Sandinista Front. I was very afraid.

"But I worked with the student movement to demand improvements there—better teachers, courses that met the needs of the Nicaraguan people. In 1971 we staged a takeover of the administration building. For that I spent two weeks in prison. After that the student movement fell apart.

"But by 1974 I had less fear. I made contact with the Front through my friend Salvador Mayorga. (Mayorga is now national director of the agrarian reform.) We worked together for a year and a half. We had a political study group, we transported arms and messages, and we hid people.

"When the Front split into three factions in 1975, I got out of touch again. But I still helped in transmitting messages. I tried to let the Front know what I thought. I always signed my messages with my code name, Pedro, and this slogan: 'Only unity will give us victory.'

"In 1976 I graduated as a lawyer but never practiced law. I went to live on the island of Solentiname in the religious community of Father Ernesto Cardenal. (Father Cardenal, once a Trappist monk at Gethsemane, Kentucky and disciple of Thomas Merton, is a noted poet and now Minister of Culture, one of several priests at the highest level of the Government of National Reconstruction.) I had met him in the university. I am a guitarist, I compose music. Maybe this is why it was easy for me to communicate with Cardenal, a poet. There I learned a lot and I experienced what it means to be part of a community.

"Then I was ready to join the armed struggle."

What was it like after Somoza fled? How did it feel the day you entered Managua victorious?

Alvaro looked at us for a long time before answering. "It was beyond description. It was the most incredible thing I've ever experienced. Everyone was in the streets. I could never relate to you what it was like. You would have had to experience it yourselves."

Men roofing a rural school house in a Miskito community near La Cruz

Jamey Stillings

Solar grain dryer at the Center for Appropriate Technology

The Peasant University

Our next stop was the Ministry of Agriculture's Center for Appropriate Technology, called the "Peasant University" by some. Like so many of the advances being made in Nicaragua today, the "university" relies on a multiplier effect. Rural communities choose representatives to study at the center; they learn a new skill on the condition that they will return home and teach it to ten others.

The students are learning by actually building the "university" itself. Under construction were handsome, one-story buildings, all made from locally available materials. In the mess hall for a lunch of beans, rice and tortillas (what else?), we noticed wall posters exhorting people to see self-discipline as part of the revolution: No smoking, Be on time for meals, Stay out of the kitchen!

First on the tour of the center's innovations were toilets designed so that the waste is used to produce biogas (to be used in cooking at the center) and organic fertilizer. The design was earthquake-proof and used local materials, our guide proudly explained. The walls were made from bricks (90 percent soil, 10 percent cement) with bamboo reinforcements.

Next we saw an earthen stove, similar in appearance to those we have seen everywhere, but this one uses only half as much wood and, to spare the cook, is designed so that the smoke is released away from where the cook is working.

Three corn cribs made out of bamboo stood on the other side of the mess hall. Traditionally peasants let corn dry in the fields; they just break the stem beneath the cob and let it hang until dry. Needless to say, pests, including rats, have a field day! These simple cribs will provide peasants a practical alternative for the first time. Made from local materials (where bamboo does not grow, other woods can be used), they are very inexpensive, last 5-10 years, and can be put up by a few neighbors helping each other. Metal cuffs around the legs, made from old tin cans with the U.S. AID handshake on them, keep rats from climbing up.

Next to the cribs was a solar grain dryer, designed so that air was heated as it passed over dark rocks. When the air reached the corn at the other end, it was hot and dry.

Before heading off again, we tried to get a sense of how those in charge of the center ended up there. Two had peasant backgrounds; they had come here to the training seminars and decided to stay. One was a civil engineer from Managua whose background was traditional building.

Another told us that he had been an agronomist for 11 years and up until a year ago had been with the agriculture ministry in Managua:

"I began to realize that Nicaragua does not have great natural resources, but our *human* resources are great. I asked for money to start an applied technology center. Here we're rediscovering from the peasants technologies that have been lost; we're not just importing ideas. We don't follow a bible, we're adapting. Every day we're learning new ways of doing things."

No doubt this group was particularly optimistic because the Dutch government had just offered a $20 million grant.

Off the Pesticide Treadmill

Our visit to the peasant university was brief because we knew that our friend Sean Swezey was waiting for us at the university in León. And we were already an hour late.

Our Institute had helped to get funds from a private donor in the States to support Sean's work. As a University of California entomologist teaching integrated pest management (IPM) at the National University in León, Sean was working to help the Nicaraguans reverse the trend that had made their country one of the pesticide capitals of the world, with thousands of poisonings each year. (See *Circle of Poison: Pesticides and People in a Hungry World,* the Institute for Food and Development Policy's book on the dumping of dangerous pesticides in the third world.)

Especially in cotton, growers had gotten locked into applying more and more pesticides as pests developed resistance. Both the foreign exchange cost and the human cost of imported pesticides had become intolerable. The pesticide contamination of mothers' milk in Nicaragua was among the highest in the world, more than ten times that considered safe in the United States.

But our first challenge was just to find Sean. University classes were to reopen the following week and remodeling was underway everywhere. The place was humming; enrollment in universities had increased over 40 percent since the overthrow of Somoza. For many, tuition was within reach for the first time.

We finally found Sean, a lanky, blond American, bubbling with enthusiasm for his work. Since we were late, he sat us right down for a slide show he had put together about pesticide use in Nicaragua.

Sean's mission is to try to help Nicaraguans get their country off the pesticide treadmill. He explained:

"Close to 90 percent of the pesticide used in the country is on cotton. Cotton was brought in here by people who said, 'We don't care about the soil, we don't care about the long-term effects on the environment, we don't care about the workers. All we care about is making a profit right now.' So, with the help of the U.S. Agency for International Development (AID) and the World Bank, a small class of growers have made themselves rich on cotton in the last 20 years.

"Pesticide applications are increasing. Recently the government prohibited the importation of any more DDT, but the stocks already here are still being used up. So, how do we get unhooked? That's what we're asking."

Sean's job is to teach the basics of pest management to students actually responsible for pest control in their work. He has 21 students, half from private farms and half pest managers on state farms. Besides teaching, Sean is an advisor to the Pilot Project for the Suppression of the Boll Weevil, directed by Nicaraguan biologist Juan Gallo.

The project involves experimenting with "cultural control" of the boll weevil, cotton's worst enemy. The technique being developed uses a "trap crop" which is planted about a month before the commercial crop. Using chemical odors called pheromones that attract the insects, thousands are diverted into the trap crop where they can be destroyed. In the battle against the boll weevil, Nicaragua has been importing insecticides and growers have been applying them as many as 40 times a season.

"Using this technique, the commercial crop will not need pesticide treatment for about 50 to 60 days. We can save six to ten applications at about 160 cordobas a throw. True, some small amount of parathion is used on the trap crop, but the entire cost is equivalent to only two applications of the commercial crop. So we still come out very far ahead.

"Based on our experiments, we could cut pesticide use in half if everyone cooperated. The key to making this work is doing it over the *whole* area, but only about 20 percent is in state farms. That means we have to have the private growers with us, really behind it. The private sector is suspicious and defensive. 'Why do you have to direct us? *We* know what to do,' is their attitude. But they are wrong; these techniques require a lot of precision. You have to plant and treat the trap crops just at the right time or the whole thing can backfire. These big growers aren't usually there when they need to be. They say they can't get their tractor out or use some other excuse not to plant the trap crop. Based on past experience, this program will never work if we leave it up to the big growers around here.

"So we're realizing that if it's going to work, the government is going to have to go in and do it as a service for the private growers. The government will say to the private growers: 'Just don't stand in our way.' It will provide the pest control service and then charge the private growers a percentage of the cost.

"In the long run it doesn't make sense to have so much of the land around here in cotton. Before the fifties when the big growers started pushing peasants off the land to grow cotton, basic grain grew here. This is good soil for basic grains. But right now the country needs the foreign exchange from exporting cotton so we can't cut back now."

Sean introduced us to Juan Gallo, director of the pilot project. "This could never have happened under Somoza," he told us. "The private producers would have blocked it. All they're interested in is short-term profit. These methods require a longer-term strategy."

The Sisters

The next morning our first stop was in Managua at one of the homes of the Maryknoll sisters, which has become virtually an alternative U.S. embassy, with so many North American delegations dropping by to get the view from the barrio.

As Sister Peggy Healy tried to answer our questions, she was pulled away to the phone half a dozen times. She had just been invited to fly with a delegation of North Americans on a fact-finding visit to the area where the government had moved about 10,000 Miskito Indians. The Nicaraguan government claimed it had to relocate the Indians because they were endangered by attacks of counterrevolutionaries based in Honduras, just across the river-border from where

Sister Peggy Healy

The reason that so many visiting Americans want to speak with the Maryknoll sisters is that many of them lived in Nicaragua before and during the insurrection. They can talk about what is going on right in the poor neighborhoods where they live and work and how it was before the revolution.

The day before, Peggy told us, she had gone with a U.S. delegation headed by Ramsey Clark, President Johnson's attorney general, to the prison where ex-National Guardsmen who had been convicted of crimes are now held.

(One of the first acts of the new government was the abolition of capital punishment. Each of the 8,000 members of Somoza's National Guard who were captured was tried. More than half were released, which outraged many of the Nicaraguans who lost loved ones to the Guard's boundless brutality. The others were imprisoned, though in 1982 the case of each prisoner was being individually reviewed for possible mistrials.)

The delegation arrived without prior notice to the prison authorities, Peggy told us, and she was impressed by what she saw. "The relationship between the guards and the prisoners seemed relaxed; the conditions seemed about as good as they could be considthe Indians lived. The U.S. government accused the Nicaraguans of horrible violations of the Indians' human rights.

ering how financially stretched the government is. I'd visited the prison a year before and the improvement was obvious. Now there are special training programs—for the ex-Guardsmen more than for the common criminals—in carpentry, shoe repair, tailoring, and TV and radio repair.

"When you see how prisoners are treated, you realize that this revolution is shot through with Christian principles. Remember that these prisoners are the universally feared and despised *Guardia* of Nicaragua's Hitler. They are people who in most countries would have been executed even without trial. But here they are individually tried and, if found guilty, given opportunities for rehabilitation. It's an incredible manifestation of Christian forgiveness."

"... *worrying about nothing*"

One of our questions about Nicaraguan development is the role of the Sandinista Defense Committees, or CDSs. The CDSs are neighborhood associations which played a big part in organizing people in working-class neighborhoods during the insurrection against Somoza. Since victory, the Sandinista leadership has seen this neighborhood organization structure as key to involving ordinary people in the development process. (The impact of the CDS organizations was highlighted during the 1982 floods when far fewer people died in Nicaragua than in neighboring Honduras, where the flooding was much less severe.)

But critics of the government view the CDS structure as just the opposite, as the embryo of totalitarian control from the top, involving neighbors "informing" on neighbors. For such critics the CDS block organizations are tools through which the Sandinistas can give orders and keep tabs on people.

We were eager to hear what Peggy thought of the CDSs.

"Anyone who is losing sleep worrying whether the CDSs are totalitarian is worrying about nothing. The CDSs started as a civil defense movement and were really strong toward the end of the war. But after triumph the CDSs waned. There was so much reconstruction work to be done and people were burned out. They were too tired to go to so many meetings!"

Another Maryknoll sister, Pat Edmiston, joined us.

"The CDSs have little ideological content," Pat explained. "From my experience, they function as a way of helping neighbors solve problems—like a cow shitting in someone's yard. People are learning some basic skills through the CDSs: even making an agenda for a meeting is a new experience for people. CDSs are the way people get together to set up a market, to figure out better bus routes, to organize vaccination and sanitary campaigns, to guarantee that everyone can buy enough of certain foods that are scarce and might otherwise be hoarded by a few. The benefits are for working people, not the well-off who whisper about totalitarianism. So you'll find CDSs functioning in the barrios but not in the upper-class neighborhoods."

Peggy continued: "The first time we saw a CDS committee form on our block was about five months ago. It organized volunteer night watches that have reduced crime a lot, not that we have violent crime here on the level we do in the States.

"After about a month and a half the CDS fell apart again. The meetings stopped. But now, because of the sugar shortage, the CDS here may get organized again. We've had periodic sugar shortages. It's hard to say how much is a real shortage and how much is due to rumors of shortages setting off hoarding. The government's trying to prevent hoarding by distributing sugar coupons to people through the block organizations. It amounts to about one pound per person per week. On our block the local restaurant owner is the head of the CDS; he took the responsibility on himself and came around to each house, taking down everyone's name."

The possibility of the CDS becoming a vehicle for control from the top did not seem a threat to Peggy. "As a force for democracy, I would like to see the CDS become much more of a channel for popular opinion.

It's starting now, but it could be much more."

Julianne Warnshuis, another Maryknoll sister, joined in our conversation. A soft-spoken blue-eyed blonde, Julianne didn't fit any stereotype of a "radical" nun either. She lives in Ciudad Sandino, which she described to us as a typical barrio of unskilled workers, unemployed people, migrant workers, some home industry and market vendors.

"It's less politicized than some barrios in Managua because it wasn't a battlefield," she explained. "When people are forced to fight for their existence, they're a lot more concerned about what comes after.

"The problem in our barrio is not really who is for or who is against the changes going on. It goes deeper. A large percentage in the barrio are not tuned in to the process of change. Historically, people feared involvement, because the forces against you were too strong and the repression could wipe out your family. Better not to get involved, better to accept conditions as they were and survive as best you could. You minded your own business. This old ethic divided people and kept them isolated—you went about life just getting as much as you could for yourself and your family.

"That has to change and it is changing. People have to come to realize that unless they get involved they'll be victimized. They must get involved so as not to be manipulated. And the CDS is a way people can get involved."

But aren't you worried that the CDS could become a tool for manipulating people?

"The CDSs have a lot of freedom about what they are supposed to be. Remember, the top isn't organized either! What I mean is that the top and the bottom (the government leadership and the grassroots organizations) are growing up at the same time. The leadership got power before they expected it. They said, 'We've won, now what do we do?' They don't have a fixed plan for how the CDSs should function. There's a lot of room for real democratic input from the bottom."

Sisters Julianne and Pat urged us to visit them in the Maryknoll house in Ciudad Sandino, where we could talk more. Peggy kept apologizing for being pulled away to the telephone every few minutes. She looked harried, exhausted. But from each of the sisters we got the clear message: there is nothing on earth they would rather be doing.

Supermarket in Managua

The Supermarket

We left the sisters and walked to the corner to take some pictures of the big supermarket. For the last few days we had been living like most Nicaraguans—in the world of beans, rice, and corn tortillas. But here we entered another world, with all the things Americans take for granted—Bel Air frozen green beans, Chivas Regal scotch, Revlon make-up and good old Sugar Frosted Flakes. There were some differences, though. On the magazine racks, right alongside *Reader's Digest*, *Mademoiselle* and *Time*, were the writings of Lenin and books on poverty in Nicaragua.

Having just driven by mile after mile of cotton fields, we examined the labels on the cotton shirts, just to see if any of them were made in Nicaragua. No—all were imported, even though so much of Nicaragua's land and human resources go to produce cotton. A powerful lesson in the legacy of underdevelopment.

We decided to talk with the store manager to find out what he thinks of the changes going on in the country and in the store. So we walked through the door at the back of the store and up the stairs. Sure enough, there was the manager's office and just the sort of person you would expect to see at a desk covered with manila folders: a middle-aged, stocky man, orderly and cordial. We explained that we were interested in Nicaragua's food system.

How has the revolution affected the store? we asked him.

"The store was bankrupt at the time of the triumph. To get it back into operation, the state financed its reopening. Now it's a joint venture—80 percent owned by the government, 20 percent private," he explained. "But this change hasn't really affected me. I have the same boss, the same employees. My salary is the same.

"What has changed a lot are our clients. We now see another class of people coming here. Many of the well-off people with a lot of purchasing power who used to shop here have left Nicaragua. Those remaining have less to spend.

"We used to have a lot of imported specialties like ham, salami, canned fruit, Danish butter cookies—things like that. But these luxury items won't be authorized in the future. The government says we can't afford these luxuries. That change will affect profits here a lot. The profit margins on the imported items are higher."

(Later Peter Marchetti explained to us that a lot of the luxury items we saw in this supermarket had been imported just before Christmas as a concession to the well-to-do. Many disagreed with the decision and Peter thought the manager was right—it will probably be the last time.)

Are there any controls on prices here?

"Oh, yes, prices of thirty basic items are controlled," the supermarket manager told us. "Things like rice, meat, corn, beans, toothpaste, and detergent. In the mom-and-pop stores the prices tend to run higher; but here the government is in control. These prices haven't risen in the last two years.

"The government maintains a good supply. In January there were days when we didn't have detergent or toothpaste . . . but you really can't call it scarcity. People create the scarcity by buying more than they need.

"So we limit the quantity that people can buy at one time of things like sugar, rice or toothpaste. Sure, people can always come back for more."

What would you do to someone who came back five times in one day, say, to buy toothpaste?

"Nothing, nothing we could do."

Can't people just go out and resell things they get cheaper here?

"Sure, it's very difficult to prevent reselling."

What about sugar? People are supposed to get coupons for sugar now. How does it work?

"Everybody has to get a card through their neighborhood organization which signs them up to get a certain amount of sugar from a store in the vicinity. It's about one pound a person a week. This has definitely reduced sugar sales. People are really angry about this. People want sugar!"

We asked about the union at the supermarket.

"Oh, yes, there had always been a union here. Since the insurrection, it's been reformed. It's more active now, but not really within the store. It's active in the militia and in the local CDS. And the union has taken on the responsibility of guarding the store at night. We don't really need it but they wanted to do it. They wanted to defend something that they say now belongs to them."

The manager seemed almost amused at the thought that the workers considered the store "theirs."

Before leaving we probed the manager's personal feelings about the changes he sees. "Frankly, we are going to be another Cuba," he said. "And the Cuban system hasn't worked there—there's no liberty and there are shortages."

We probed a little deeper. We told him that we had spoken with many of the Sandinista leaders and they say they're trying specifically to *avoid* being like Cuba. (Even Fidel Castro has warned the Nicaraguans not to institute many of the policies he did.)

"The Sandinistas are just hiding their true goals because they have to live alongside the United States," he said firmly.

Then why do you stay?

"Because for me everything is the same as before. Personally, I have no problem with the new govern-ment. I'm the same as always. I've no reason to leave."

We are aware, of course, that this supermarket manager could be correct: if enough external pressure is exerted against Nicaragua's economy—as the United States is trying to do—controls on consumption could become tighter. If the external threats, including ter-rorist attacks, intensify, internal liberties will prob-ably be curtailed. But what struck us most about this supermarket manager is that he seemed so certain about something that he himself had not experienced. Our hunch is that his assumptions have been heavily influenced by propaganda, beginning long before the overthrow of Somoza, which paints the Sandinistas as hard-line, immoral communists.

The peasants we spoke with in Santa Maria had been influenced by the same propaganda, but their ideas are changing now that they are experiencing big changes in their lives. This manager's life has not changed—and neither have his views.

Pantipitu community in front of Moravian chapel

Jamey Stillings

"How do peasants become revolutionaries?"

That afternoon we had the chance to look more closely at the roots of the Nicaraguan revolution. We had been struck that so many people we had met had been deeply influenced in their commitment to social change by the Catholic Church—Caliche as a teenager, Alvaro on the island retreat with Father Cardenal, the Maryknoll sisters, and of course Peter—Father Marchetti—our guide. But exactly how did the Church in Nicaragua go from being a legitimizer of the status quo to a vital impetus for change?

At the headquarters of the Educational Center for Agrarian Advancement (known as CEPA), we met Justinian Liebel. He had spent 25 years as a Capuchin priest in the eastern half of Nicaragua—in what he

Justinian Liebel

called the "bush"—working with the poorest of Nicaraguans. For two hours we sat talking in the courtyard near an empty swimming pool—for this center, like so many of the offices we visited, had once been the luxury home of a Somocista.

"It all started with a fateful decision the Church made in 1965, Justinian explained. "The Church opened the window on what it previously had condemned—a lay priesthood, what came to be known throughout Latin America as the Delegates of the Word. After 1968, the whole Church in Latin America gradually became involved in promoting "grassroots communities" (*comunidades de base*), each led by a Delegate of the Word.

"A growing number of priests encouraged the poor communities to study the meaning of the Word of God as it applies to the conditions of their own daily lives. Through informal talks in people's homes, leaders were developed and came forward, and they became the Delegates. The Church began bringing these leaders into the towns for courses in the New Testament.

"Just as important, in 1968 the American Bible Society published the New Testament in modern Spanish and in paperback. These Bibles started selling in the bush for one cordoba apiece. For the first time, many people started reading the Bible. The language was simple. They could understand.

"Now in the coastal and central regions of the country we have about 1,000 communities led by Delegate couples, a husband and wife who share the responsibility. Every Sunday they hold a Celebration of the Word. They prepare the people for baptism and matrimony. And out of these communities came other leaders, in health and agriculture, for instance.

"The Jesuit Fathers founded the Educational Center for Agrarian Advancement in 1972 to provide services to these communities, to give courses to some of these new rural leaders and to provide some teaching materials.

"Another influence was the work of Paulo Freire, the Brazilian teacher who wrote *The Pedagogy of the Oppressed.* His work helped us develop a new vision of Christ, a Christ present in service. We learned and we taught that to be a Christian you have to be free to make your own choices. With this consciousness, we kept asking ourselves, how should we respond to what we hear on the radio about the revolutionary struggle against the dictatorship?

"And that was another thing—the radio," Justinian continued. "People rarely mention this but an important part of the revolution was the 'transistor revolution.' It really hit about 1960-62. Before, on my long rides through the bush I had a lot of time to talk with people. I would chat about other countries, about snow, about the ocean—anything outside their daily experience and they thought I was crazy! But then radio came. They'd have it on day and night. They started learning about the world. Their mentality started to change."

How did you help people apply the Bible in their own lives? we asked.

"We taught a week's course, for example, on the Maccabees. It is about the Jewish people being exterminated by Greek culture. The Maccabees clung to what they believed in. Then we would ask: Does this story reflect anything happening to you today?

"We taught the Apocalypse. It is a book written in code. It tells of the persecution of the Church. Then we would ask: How would *you* write the story of your life in code?

"The Sandinista Front has said that if it weren't for this kind of consciousness raising by the Delegates, the revolution could not have succeeded. Needless to say, the Delegates became a target of the marauding Guard."

Our conversation then turned to the reports of the conflict between the government and the Miskito Indians on the Atlantic coast. Justinian explained that most of the Miskitos had never identified with the Sandinista-led revolution. They always saw it as just "Spaniards fighting Spaniards," since the Indian people have completely different languages and cultures. The Sandinistas were not sensitive to those differences, according to Justinian, creating hostility toward the government.

"Remember that when the Sandinistas came to power at most only a few hundred people had any real leadership experience and enough education to handle the top administrative jobs. Yet they had to rebuild the entire country overnight! Who's going to handle the garbage collection? Who's going to create a police department? And education and health? They had almost nobody.

"There were very few Sandinistas prepared to work on the Atlantic Coast. Only 10 percent of the people live there and, like most Nicaraguans, the Sandinistas knew little about it. So it was a low priority. And the inexperienced youths they sent out to the Atlantic Coast made some horrible mistakes that will take ten years to correct. They were overbearing and arrogant and pushed people around, with little consideration for different cultures, languages, and customs.

"Aided by outside help, the ex-National Guardsmen along the Honduran side of the Rio Coco, the river marking the Nicaragua-Honduras border, manipulated some Miskitos. Plans to invade Nicaraguan territory on a big scale with the help of local Miskitos were uncovered. Along the entire border area, invading forces from Honduras were robbing, killing, and generally vandalizing the population during the last half of 1981.

In December 1981, the government uncovered a well developed plan called "Red Christmas" to attack

across the Rio Coco and cut off a section of Nicaraguan
territory. The government countered by declaring the
entire Rio Coco area military territory. They decided to
evacuate the banks of the Rio Coco so the national
territory could be defended militarily and to relocate
the Miskitos to new lands to protect their lives. The
relocation took place in January 1982. The government made every effort to do it well and they did a good
job under very difficult conditions. With the people
relocted in "Tasba Pri" (The Free Land), they are putting in a tremendous amount of supplies and well-
trained people to help the Miskitos from the Rio Coco
build a new life, secure from the threats of the counterrevolutionaries in Honduras."

Can they pull it off?

"Personally, I think they can. If they could pull off
the last two and a half years . . . just keeping the
country going is a miracle!"

But many Americans dismiss the good intentions
of the Sandinistas because they are waiting until 1985
to hold elections.

"I went through 25 years of Somoza elections,"
Justinian told us. "They were one big farce. Nicaraguans
have never had a free election. Elections have no
meaning as long as people are illiterate and ignorant of
the what the elections mean. Remember Nicaragua is
still two-thirds rural—and I mean *bush.* Sure, illiteracy
is down. Still, most people are not functionally literate
. . . I mean buying newspapers and books. You don't
solve these problems in two and a half years. All you
can do is begin a process.

"Sure, I'm not blind to this government's problems.
But it is a great thing happening here. . . ."

How are People Eating?

Leaving Justinian, we headed back to the Center for the Study of the Agrarian Reform (CIERA), the research arm of the Ministry of Agriculture where Peter works. There we met several Americans, a Frenchman and an Englishman, all there in technical and advisory roles. We wanted to ask questions about their ongoing study of Nicaragua's food system. So the group in charge of the study—two Nicaraguans, one Englishman, and one American—invited us to supper. We gathered at a simple outdoor restaurant.

As they explained their work, it dawned on us once again how underdevelopment means starting from scratch. In this case we learned that it means that even the most rudimentary data on people's food needs was

Tienda Popular in Managua

not available to the government. Yet without this information, how can the government plan effective food strategies?

The job of these young people—the Food System Study Team—is to provide the basic data, not just on how people are eating, but how people view their food problems and what they want done.

"We're starting with a series of case studies," the Englishman, Peter Utting, explained to us. "We selected ten barrios in Managua, each one representing a somewhat different income level. First, we ask the neighborhood organizations, the CDSs, to call a general neighborhood meeting for everyone to talk about their problems. In these meetings we can get a pretty good sense of people's experience—what they eat, where they buy their food, why they buy it where they do, how they think food distribution should be organized. Then we ask people to meet with us individually the next day."

What are you finding? How do people respond?

"Most of the people say that for them, the situation is more or less the same as before the start of the revolution. We're not surprised. Some say it is worse. Some say they are eating about the same but it's better now because the government is doing something."

Why do you say that you're not surprised?

"Because the country's still recovering. Food production was wiped out during the insurrection and it's taking time to rebuild. Last year the government increased the credit to small farmers who produce most of the country's beans and corn. It was almost five times what they ever got under Somoza. Production did go up, but transportation to get the food from the countryside into the city was inadequate. A lot of the food rotted. And we had to import food. This year it will be better, definitely. For the first time in many years, we shouldn't need to import.

"But an even harder problem is that families without regular employment obviously still have a rough time of it. And at the same time, with more money among the less well-off, there's the release of pent-up desires for more food and especially for meat; the result is higher prices, which shut many people out."

At the ENABAS store in Santa Maria we had seen one example of how the government is trying to help make basic foods available to the poor at controlled prices. We were curious about how this system was working in Managua, the capital.

Are efforts like ENABAS' what the people mean when they say that at least the government is doing something to help now?

"Yes, exactly. The government is trying a number of things in the poor barrios of the city. It is contracting with one or two of the mom-and-pop stores (*pulperias*) in the barrio who will get the basic foods through ENABAS if they pledge to sell them at the fixed retail prices. The local CDS usually selects the store on the basis of the owners' honesty and refusal to raise prices when something is in scarce supply.

"The government is also setting up its own outlets (*tiendas populares*) in the poor neighborhoods—so far about 40. The latest idea is mobile units, trucks that go out to the more marginal settlements to sell the basic foods to people."

All this conversation about the poor's access to

corn and beans took place as we enjoyed the delicious burritos with sour cream and fresh mango and yogurt drinks. We realized that while most people of the world feel blessed if they have access to just three or four basic foods, we Americans feel deprived if we have to eat the same thing for dinner two nights in a row.

The Food System Study Team asked us if we wanted to join them that evening in one of the poorest barrios in Managua. The CDS there had agreed to call a special meeting in which people would answer questions about their food problems as part of the survey. Of course we accepted.

It was dark as we drove into the barrio, right on the shore of Lake Managua. About 25 people, mostly women, were sitting in an open area outside someone's home. A single light bulb swung in the breeze, making our shadows dance. We sat on a low-hanging limb; others sat on boxes and many just stood. (A friend had explained to us why most CDS meetings were held outside: if held inside, it was easier for those who didn't come to imagine that their neighbors were using the meetings to spread rumors about them.)

Sonia, one of the Nicaraguan members of the survey team, led the discussion while the other three took notes. Sonia went down each major food—corn, beans, rice, meat etc.—skillfully asking how much people ate, where they shopped, why and so on.

She joked with the people, making a point of calling on individuals by name and doing what good "facilitators" are supposed to do. People did have a lot of complaints. They clearly didn't think they were benefitting much from the government stores and didn't like the coupon system for distributing sugar.

Commented one woman: "Everyone's talking about the sugar shortage. Everyone's upset. When you go to the movie you can't even hear the movie because everyone's talking about sugar!"

We weren't particularly surprised by people's complaints, since we assumed there would be a huge gap between the government's plans for helping people and people actually feeling helped. So we were surprised the next day when Sonia told us her impressions. She was very upset. She said that they had organized such meetings in seven or eight neighborhoods so far and had never heard so many complaints.

Sonia explained that the meeting had drawn together people who really came from two different communities within the barrio—one moderately poor, the other very poor, what she called *la miseria*. They had different interests. The women in the poorer community had asked the government for a state store. But two small merchants from the somewhat better-off community also came to the meeting were somewhat better off, and they felt threatened by the store.

Sonia was shocked that people were so critical of

the coupon system for sugar. "This is the opposite reaction to what we had seen in other barrios. The CDSs were involved in developing the sugar coupon system to avoid hoarding. Most of them are behind it."

But the biggest shock to Sonia seemed to be people's reaction to the ENABAS store (the government outlet for basic foods). They weren't using these stores. "Why?" we asked.

"Because these people are *so* poor they can't buy anything in quantity," Sonia told us. "The ENABAS store sells food by the pound but these people are so poor they have to buy a little food each day, just enough to get by—maybe one cup of rice, a little oil—like that. So they go to the mom-and-pop store. Sure it's more expensive but they can buy a little at a time. Also they can get credit there."

Sonia was shaken. The system the government had devised to help the poor in Managua was apparently not reaching the neediest as well as expected. Suddenly it seemed more difficult than she had imagined.

Neighborhood Democracy

We drove to a working-class barrio of Managua where we had been invited to attend a regular meeting of CDS coordinators. Here the leaders of each block group from the barrio come together. When we arrived, the meeting was well underway. A friend living in the barrio had already explained who we were so no one paid much attention as we took our seats.

Mostly we wanted just to get a feeling for how decisions were made and who these grassroots leaders were. They were quite a mix, men and women, from teenage to middle age. They represented twelve CDSs, each covering one to three blocks—about 538 people.

We came in in the middle of a discussion of what role the CDS coordinators should play in helping to mobilize people for the coming commemoration of one of the most popular martyrs of the revolution, Carlos Fonseca, a founder of the Sandinista Liberation Front killed several years before victory.

Like so many meetings of our Institute back in San Francisco, the atmosphere was charged as people debated their ideas. The free-wheeling discussion went round and round, but after 15 or 20 minutes a consensus emerged. There was no vote; the chair simply summed up his understanding of the consensus and asked if anyone disagreed. No one did.

The next item was the dance planned for Saturday night. The music was the only problem left. The chair suggested they rent equipment at 100 cordobas an hour. But the leader's idea was immediately rejected. "No, no, too much money." A woman then volunteered her father's sound equipment—"but only if one person will take responsibility for it." After a lot of joking about who was to be the "slave" to sit by the equipment, a young man volunteered. "I don't dance, so I'll do it," he offered.

Before the meeting closed, there was a chance for people to talk about the things most troubling them.

A woman in her forties told the group that she was upset because "we don't even have a photo of William Diaz Romero" in the CDS coordinating center. The center was named for him since he was one of the young people from the neighborhood killed during the insurrection.

"We should have a photo gallery of all our fallen," she scolded the group. "And our streets. We have named these streets for our martyrs but we don't even use the names!"

A young man then asked the group to send a telegram to the radio stations, declaring their support for the government in an upcoming meeting of the Socialist International, the coordinating body of the world's democratic socialist parties. But no action was taken; others said they needed to find out more about the meeting first.

A young woman then spoke out about her disappointment at the lack of progress on the library they'd begun. "We made the decision almost a month ago but still there are not enough books," she said. "And there are only five or six books about Nicaragua! People haven't contributed books the way they were supposed to. And we haven't made a card catalog." The others nodded in agreement but we wondered if her pleas would make any difference.

"Any more points?" asked the chair.

Another middle-aged woman spoke up. She told of an incident the night before while she was on the volunteer street crime patrol organized by a CDS.

"Two young men came up to us and starting throwing stones," she explained. "They were drunk and yelled horrible things. They said bad things about Tomás Borge (the only surviving founder of the Sandinista Front and a very popular government leader). Then they showed us papers proving they were members of the Sandinista Youth. But I can't believe that members of the Sandinista Youth would be creating such a ruckus in the street and putting down the Revolution!"

In the discussion that ensued some suspected that the young rabblerousers were infiltrators—counterrevolutionaries who had infiltrated the Sandinista organizations.

"You should have followed them to find out who they are," one man offered. "But we have to carry out our viligance in a good way or we will alienate people and be helping the reactionaries," another warned.

The meeting was spontaneous, with much lively debate. The leader was not in control or even particularly deferred to. Some of the issues dealt with were those that a block group here in the United States might take up—a neighborhood dance, for example. Others, such as the vaccination campaigns or sugar distribution, involve the CDS in important responsibilities.

On the other hand, the discussion about suspected infiltrators did make us apprehensive. We know that in any society feeling its survival threatened people become suspicious of each other. Some will be attacked unjustly as when the U.S. government locked Japanese-Americans into camps and seized their property in the aftermath of Pearl Harbor. Others will become afraid to disagree with the majority view. Nicaragua's notable openness could change quickly in response to continued U.S. hostility and armed attacks from Honduras.

"People can come and say what they want . . . "

At the meeting's close, we asked if anyone would be willing to stay and talk with us about the role of the CDSs. It was after 10, late for a country where most people are up before 6. Still, three men stayed for at least an hour more.

As we talked, we watched out of the corners of our eyes as several members pitched in to whip the library into shape. They organized the books and labeled the shelves. We were impressed, especially because the hour was so late. We felt a little ashamed that we had assumed the earlier criticism wouldn't have any effect on the foot dragging.

Of the three who stayed behind to talk with us, the most outspoken was David. He couldn't have been more than twenty. David reminded us that the CDSs were born during the revolutionary struggle to support the guerillas but, just as important, to provide for the needs of the community in the liberated zones. "Without the CDSs we would have died of hunger; we would have had no medicines."

In David's view the CDSs initiate projects, as well as help carry out programs organized by the various social ministries—such as the vaccination campaigns, the literacy campaign, etc.

"The CDSs recently proposed to the government that we take responsibility for distributing sugar to avoid hoarding. The CDSs are making sure that not a single family in the country is without sugar."

What else do the CDSs do?

"Urban improvements like garbage cans, organizing celebrations, helping improve the mass transit so people can get to work easier. And we also have political education."

What is political education?

"We have a political seminar every Wednesday evening for whomever wants to come," David explained. "Sometimes government leaders come in to talk with us, sometimes someone from the barrio with special knowledge. We've had discussions on the role of the Church, on the role of political parties.

"Sometimes someone from the government comes to present a law that is being considered in the Council of State. Like the Paternity Law last year. Every single committee of the barrio collected information on how people felt about the proposed paternity law. (The law would assign legal responsibility to fathers to support their children. About 40 percent of Nicaragua households are headed by women.) The heads of each of the block level CDSs sent these results to the zone level. They compiled their results and sent them to the province level and on up. "When the discussions started, there were a lot of differences. But we talked and talked and people wound up agreeing a lot.

"Another example of laws we've discussed in the CDS is the Agrarian Reform Law," said David. "But maybe the most involved was the National Consultation on Education. The Ministry of Education pub-

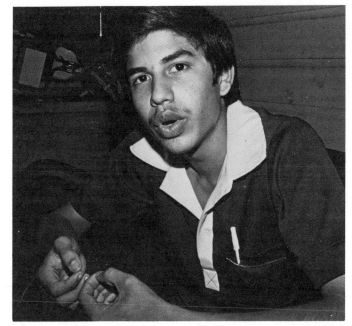

David

lished a discussion guide with lots of questions about the kind of education people want for Nicaragua. It was discussed at every level—in schools, in offices, and in the neighborhoods.

"The views brought out in these discussions will be the basis of the new education in Nicaragua. Before, education was just for the minority. And you didn't learn to think; you just repeated things. You didn't learn anything about the economy. The books were appropriate for industrial countries; they didn't take into account the reality of our country. All the science was theoretical, not practical. And you had to study English. If you failed English, you failed all the subjects. So I didn't really have a chance to develop myself."

We then turned the conversation to questions we know are in the minds of so many skeptics of the CDS form of participation. Won't the CDSs turn out to be tools for keeping dissent under control, vehicles for neighbors to spy on each other?

"My answer is based on the meeting we just had. People can come and say what they want," David replied. "If people are attacking the organizations working for the benefit of the people, it's because they've been negatively affected by propaganda, like *La Prensa*'s. (*La Prensa*, whose former editor was assassinated by Somoza's henchmen, is now filled with what many observers see as distortions, sensationalism, and vitriolic attacks on the new government.) Take transportation. *La Prensa* tries to make people believe that the transportation problem is a government problem. But 95 percent of the mass transit is private! And two of the unions who are against the government have blown up buses. And then they blame the government for problems."

We told David about the woman in the marketplace who was hostile to the Sandinista government. "She wanted to be left alone," we said.

"There is so much work to be done," he said. "It's logical after two and a half years that people feel bothered. There is so much to learn; it takes a lot of discipline—the vaccination campaigns, literacy, working to control corruption, sometimes standing in line. Some people feel like they are being pressured."

David seemed to accept this as part of the given. Even if it's for good ends, not everybody will want to change.

"But what about elections?" we asked. "At home, people say that if the Sandinistas were truly for democracy, they would have held elections by now."

"We had elections under Somoza. Those fighting for elections now want to go back to the past. More important is who holds power. And now the people hold power."

How?

"One way is through the CDSs. Through them we

elect nine members to the Council of State. Each year popular assemblies meet to elect our delegates."

But critics of the Nicaraguan system of democracy charge that the CDS seats on the Council of State are simply a way for the government to pack the Council with representatives loyal to it. We planned to take up this question with a member of the Council.

State textile factory, Managua

Alvaro Arguello

"Defining the rules of the game"

The next morning we arrived at the Central American Historical Institute to meet its director, Alvaro Arguello. The Institute is a nongovernmental research and educational organization studying developments in Central America. It is funded by private sources, including some European groups.

Arguello, a Jesuit priest, is also an elected member of Nicaragua's Council of State. On the rare occasions when it is mentioned in U.S. media, it is insinuated that the Council is mere window-dressing for a "Marxist dictatorship."

We were, therefore, delighted to be meeting someone who we hoped could help us assess the reality of the Council. Alvaro, a distinguished-looking man in

his late forties, greeted us in his office, which looked more like a library: every inch of the walls was covered with shelves of books and papers.

Alvaro began by impressing upon us that the Council of State was not thrown up overnight as a last minute afterthought once the Sandinistas came to power.

"Planning for the Council of State started months before victory by the leadership in exile in Costa Rica," he explained. From the beginning it was seen "as a way to involve people from all social groups—groups which had contributed to the toppling of Somoza in different ways—in shaping the future of Nicaragua. The philosophy was that the state is to be a tool of the people. But how do we make the association between the people and the state? In Nicaragua this is no longer just a theory: the Council of State translates this theory into reality."

But who is the Council of State? we interjected.

"Thirty-two organizations have representatives on the Council of State. There are 51 people. Each of the organizations can decide itself how to select its representatives. Five types of organizations make up the Council: political parties, popular organizations like the woman's organization and the organization of neighborhood groups (CDS), unions, professional associations and the churches, and private enterprise. I was elected to represent the Nicaraguan Association of Catholic Clergy."

What power does the Council have?

The Council has "colegislative" powers with the three-person junta to create the basic institutions of a new Nicaraguan society, Alvaro explained. He drew the lines of a baseball diamond in the air—baseball is a popular sport in Nicaragua and the U.S. major leagues are avidly followed even by the Sandinista press. The Council of State, Alvaro continued, serves "to lay out the rules of the game, just as kids might take an empty lot and mark it off with stones as bases, saying 'this is where we are going to play.' "

And what are the rules?

"The rules of the game include pluralism and national unity, but underlying these goals is one more basic rule that underlies everything—the satisfaction of the basic needs of the majority, for example, for food, health and housing. This comes before all else. This is the axis on which all else will be constructed. This is the one direction toward which we will move all the resources we have. *Within* this, not outside this, we will have pluralism and an economy with both private and public ownership.

"This is the historical right of this revolution. For centuries, since the time of the conquistadors, the government has failed the majority. To renounce this opportunity now would be to renounce our historical experience, to renounce the blood shed by 50,000 Nicaraguans, mainly young people."

Alvaro spoke eloquently and with great confidence —not at all defensively.

As if he were sensing our difficulty in understanding these concepts, he continued, "There is no model to fall back on to try to understand what we are doing. It is a process; it is not fixed. We can't use models such as the liberal French Revolution or the system of 'checks and balances.' They are good theories but they don't apply here.

"Other countries have hurt Nicaragua by trying to impose their models of government. Many are pressuring us to have elections now—and not just the U.S. but many countries. But we intend our elections to have real meaning for the people.

"After so many coups d'etat there have been elections. What have they meant? In some cases following a military coup the government has stayed in for years before announcing elections. In Honduras it was ten years. But here, only one year and one month after triumph the government at least three times formally announced that elections will be held, not in ten years but in 1985 and with campaigning to start in 1984. And this in spite of the fact that we are starting from zero—creating a whole new structure.

"So I'm astonished to see the U.S. come down on Nicaragua, cut off aid, promote counterrevolutionary bands, and classify Nicaragua as totalitarian. This shows its ideological bias."

Alvaro then proceeded to explain to us how the legislative process works in Nicaragua.

"There are two institutions in Nicaragua with legislative power—the Council of State and the Junta of the Government of National Reconstruction. They are linked and both have the power to initiate legislation. In most cases each must pass its initiative through the other. But in certain areas the Junta has exclusive authority; in others the Council of State does.

"When a law is initiated in the Council of State, first it is passed to a committee for study—much like in your Congress. Then it is debated in the Council and, if approved in a roll call vote, the law then passes to the Junta which can either accept it and publish it as law or, if they disagree, can return it to the Council of State with suggested changes. The Junta can also pass it into law but tell the Council the reasons why they don't think it is a good law."

How does this work in practice? Does the Council of State really have independent views?

"Take the law of eminent domain, for example. There was a lot of debate. One of the contributions of the Council of State was to add in compensation to owners whose property was affected. The Council of State thought the draft law was too inflexible. The draft called for payment in state bonds. But who knows what they'll be worth? The Council pushed for a more flexible policy—using cash or bonds depending on the situation. The Council wanted direct negotiations, case by case, instead of just an inflexible formula. And the Council's position became law.

"There was another law regarding the confiscation of factories where the owners are draining capital out of the country. The Council of State added into the law that workers were prohibited from taking over factories. And the Junta approved it. This might look like the Council was against the workers. But the objective of the law was to take into account the needs of the whole economy. Other laws, of course, have directly favored workers.

"There is a lot of back and forth. In practice it's working very well. It works well because the Council is a political forum for debates involving conflicting interests."

You mentioned that certain areas are exclusively in the hands of the Junta. What are they?

"First is the budget. Other areas include the organization of ministries of government, naming of high government officials, declaring state of emergencies, international treaties, and foreign credits."

In what areas does the Council of State have exclusive authority?

"The Council is empowered to come up with the electoral law and the constitution. The electoral law will determine which posts will be open for election and which will be appointed. The Council of State also ratifies international treaties. It defines citizenship and is responsible for laws about national symbols.

"The Council can also demand reports from ministers and other officials. Let me give you an example. I'm sure you've heard about our sugar 'shortage.' Well, we asked the Minister of Internal Commerce to come to us and explain just how this could happen. There have been seven or eight cases like this."

If the Council of State is in session only from May to December, what happens when it's not in session?

"During recess we can be called back. In fact, right now we have been called back to discuss the very important law on political parties. It's up to the president of the Council of State to fix the date for such debate."

Critics of Nicaragua would say that the Council is a tool of the Junta because it is the Junta that decides how many delegates from each sector—and the majority are from pro-Sandinista popular organizations, not business groups. What do you say to such critics?

"Of course the Junta decides. It would not reflect the reality of political life now to think it wouldn't. They, the Sandinistas, won the victory over Somoza, for they succeeded in uniting and guiding the great majority of Nicaragua's social sectors. So it would be against historical reality to deny them the right to exercise hegemony at this time."

But your critics see this power as totalitarianism. . .

"Do you appreciate that one of the very special qualities of this revolution is its *generosity*? It offers all political parties the chance to prove by their actions what they say. The other parties, even the Conservative Party, say they are for the revolution, that they took part in the war against Somoza. We'll let them prove it. This revolution gives an opportunity to all political parties to help build a new society. It is up to them to participate or not. Several, including some communist organizations, have chosen not to participate in the process within the rules of the game I mentioned earlier."

We asked Alvaro about the path he had traveled to his present involvement in the Nicaraguan revolution.

"I was born in 1933. A product of a Jesuit high school in Granada, Nicaragua, I studied as a Jesuit seminarian in El Salvador, Ecuador, Spain, France, and Kansas. As a priest, I was in the graduate program in science at Rutgers University in New Jersey. From 1974 on, I've run the Institute. But what has most shaped my perception of developments today is that starting in 1977 I and some other Jesuits have been living in direct contact with the poor in what today is called Ciudad Sandino. We followed the people. They helped us understand the national reality. Side by side with them we experienced the insurrection of September 1978 and the repression of Somoza's *Guardia.* We learned and, I think, we continue to learn."

How do you see the future? What do you see after 1985?

"There will be more popular participation, surely. People will have had more experience. But it is difficult to foresee the future. That is the nature of a revolutionary process."

Then Alvaro paused. "Of course, by 1985 we may be fighting against invasion."

New housing project for 1000 workers, Managua

"We could have lived comfortably"

Father Arguello had just told us that the axis on which the new Nicaragua is to be built is the fulfillment of the basic needs for the country's poor and hungry. He saw himself engaged in political decisions toward that end. Our next stop was the Ministry of Planning where we met a woman helping make economic decisions toward the same end.

Like most of the government offices we'd seen, the building hardly looked governmental. It looked like a barracks or low-priced motel with rooms stretched along walkways, opening out on a courtyard. In this makeshift arrangement we found Malena de Montis, head of the section of the planning ministry which evaluates how the country is achieving the goal of meeting the basic needs of the people.

Malena de Montis

We immediately liked her. In her mid-thirties, Malena's face was relaxed and warm. Her manner was professional but not the least stuffy. She was the first woman we had met in an official government post, although women are a substantial portion of the leadership except in the very highest level of the government.

What in your life led you to be in this position today? we asked.

"My life was very privileged. I studied in private schools. I studied in the United States—at Immaculate Heart College in Pennsylvania and at Florida State University.

"But from my very early years I became sensitive to the poverty of the people. My father was a civil engineer, a naturalized American citizen. He built roads, and during the summertime we would travel with him into the countryside. I could see the terrible poverty.

"As a teenager I studied in a school run by the Maryknoll Sisters in Guatemala. On weekends we did social work. So I was always in contact with different realities. The contrasts were just too strong. I knew I couldn't go on living with such levels of injustice and misery.

"It was only after I became an adult that I began to learn about the history of Nicaragua. In schools very little is taught about our history. For me, Sandino had been a bandit. That's what they taught us. Books that said anything else were prohibited.

"There are lots of us with similar experience. We could have lived very comfortably. But the contrasts were just too strong. The suffering was so visible. We could have lived very comfortably but always confronted by beggars.

"For a lot of us, the religious community played a big role in our lives. It is within the religious framework that we became aware.

"Another important influence on us was the incredible corruption within the upper class. Their social life was disgusting. And today their children are rebelling against that type of life. I don't want to overdo it, but there is an element of psychological rebellion against their parents' disgusting values."

When did you actually get involved in the revolution?

"I got in touch with the Sandinistas when I was living in Panama, working in planning. I began to do solidarity work in Costa Rica and I also worked in Europe to get support for the Sandinistas. I didn't come back to Nicaragua until the 20th of July."

On July 19, 1979, the victorious Sandinista Front marched into Managua. Hundreds of Nicaraguans rushed back to help build the new country. What was it like then?

"It has been a very difficult struggle. Remember that the great majority of us have had no experience in administration. One of our greatest handicaps is our inexperience. Sure, I worked in planning in Panama but doing very limited studies. For us, the big change is that now we're in charge!

"At the department of social programs, our job is to try to expand social services—health, education, access to drinking water and so on—and to try to evaluate just how well all the government programs are meeting people's needs."

But with such limited funds, what can the government do?

"Progress will depend a lot on what the people themselves can do. We are trying to link up the initiatives of the popular organizations, like the adult education program and the neighborhood organizations, with the limited help the government can offer. We are trying to use them as structures for participation and popular power.

"For example, we're asking: "How can the adult education program be linked to training people for productive activities? How can they become structures for people to learn about first aid, basic health, nutrition? To start gardens or day care centers?

"We would like the adult education centers to become a springboard to the development of cooperatives. How could they become centers where people could learn more skills for building cooperatives? These are some of the questions we are asking.

"The first step is to find out more about the people who just learned to read and write—those in the adult education program. So right now we are designing a survey to develop occupational profiles of them, to find out what is their level of technical training. Once we have these profiles, then we can develop a technical package that will respond to their needs.

"Of course all of this is very intimately linked to the agrarian reform, which is providing people with land for the first time and encouraging cooperatives."

Even though you have said that the government must depend on the initiatives of the people, what can you tell us about the allocation of government money for social development now, compared to under Somoza?

"Well, remember that under Somoza the ministries of social welfare or culture didn't even exist! In real terms I can tell you that we have doubled national expenditures for education and health.

"Our big job in the Ministry of Planning is to try to give some direction and priorities to the institutions involved in providing the basic needs. We're trying to study now just how the basic needs of the urban sector are being met. But it is so difficult. We don't have the income data we need. We have only a very inadequate 11-year-old census.

How do you respond to attacks on Nicaragua that suggest you are setting up a Marxist state modeled after Cuba or the Soviet Union?

"We've always been very conscious that we have to bring about something unique to us—something that is *ours.* Of course, we also will try to learn from all the movements that are trying to free themselves and working for justice.

"I am astonished by your government's enormous hostility towards us. It presents a deformed vision which has a big impact here, too. Every hour, more propaganda against what we are trying to do. Our work is hard; this makes it even harder."

Salvador Mayorga

New Hope in the Countryside

It was almost dinner time when we reached the office of Salvador Mayorga, the director of Nicaragua's agrarian reform. Like Alvaro Reyes, Malena de Montis and so many of the government officials we met, Salvador is in his early thirties, unassuming, and direct.

"We started the agrarian reform on the basis of a decree that took less than a single sheet of paper!" he told us. "What we've been doing since is developing a judicial framework. Reality has been moving much faster than the law."

Salvador was referring to the fact that Nicaragua's first act of agrarian reform was a simple decree that farms abandoned by Somoza and his close allies were the property of the new government. (Generally large, mechanized operations, they were made into state farms. The government feared that breaking them up would undermine production.) The Law of Agrarian Reform, developed over the first two years, was announced in July 1981. The law guarantees individual property rights but only as long as the owner productively uses the land. [See our book *What Difference Could a Revolution Make? Food and Farming in the New Nicaragua.*]

"Sometimes I have been surprised—and a little worried, too—at what we have been able to develop with no experience," Salvador told us. "I've talked with people who participated in the Chilean agrarian reform law, under the Christian Democrats and then under Allende's government. They had enormous teams of scholars and experts dedicating a great deal of time to analyzing the agrarian reality and developing the laws.

"We think we've been able to pull this off because of the mix of ideas and experience of people all over the country. Our ministry worked up the first draft with the union of small farmers and ranchers and the farmworkers association. We circulated it through their regional offices where they held working sessions on the law. All comments were collected and brought to the ministry. We consulted with concerned people—for example, leaders in the revolution who had experience with peasants and farmworkers.

"Once we had a law drafted we announced the general points last summer at the celebration of the second anniversary of the revolution. Then it went to the Council of State where amendments were proposed—very few, really.

"One of the areas of debate over the Agrarian Reform Law was compensation to owners when idle land is taken. In our original proposal they would have received compensation. But the Council said owners of idle land should *not* get compensation. On review-ing this, the Junta said no—we must give compensation. We sent the law back to the Council who came up with a compromise, the plan to compensate owners of idle land with a type of bond that is less valuable than the bonds offered to owners who are just underutilizing their land. But we all agreed on no compensation for abandoned farms.

"There was a lot of debate in the Council. Just to give you an idea—my uncle was on the Council, head of one of the conservative parties. He died recently. He wanted to give compensation to all the landowners—even those who abandoned their land. And he wanted to shield owners of idle land. The law says that you are subject to having your land taken if you have 850 acres or more lying idle anywhere—cumulative total. My uncle wanted to change this to at least 850 acres in any one place. At the other extreme was the Communist Party, which opposed compensation for anyone."

What was the reaction of the small farmers and the farm laborers to the new law?

"Well, since their organizations were involved in developing it, there was little criticism. Only little things. In fact, the law was presented jointly by the ministry and the unions of the small farmers and the farmworkers."

And what has been the reaction of the big producers?

"They were never radically against the law. In off-the-record conversations they admitted that the law was very realistic. It is much more moderate than they had expected. They compared it with what the U.S. has pushed in El Salvador. At least on paper, the El Salvador law is more sweeping.

"Since the law was passed, the big growers have been scrambling not to come under the terms of the law. They've quickly tried to protect their abandoned land. They rushed to the bank to get credit to plant the most visible part or put some cattle on it.

"But it hasn't all been just for appearances. Generally there has been a positive reaction. Although, of course, some are anxious."

With the compensation you are offering, would someone be able to survive?

"Let me give you an example. A medium-sized producer with 600 idle manzanas might be offered 3,000 cordobas for each manzana. He would get a 1.8 million cordoba bond at 4 percent interest which would provide 6,000 cordobas a month income. That's the salary of a middle range government functionary.

"The law is flexible. Say someone has three or four farms which are very unproductive. By law we could take them all. But we might suggest that the owner keep one and put all his effort into that one.

"In the case of older people who rent out their land, we might pay partly in bonds and partly in cash so that they have sufficient income for the rest of their lives.

"So now some of the big landowners are coming to us with proposals. Three months ago we got a letter from an owner of 30,000 manzanas, almost entirely idle. He made some proposals to us and we have in turn made some to him.

"In another case of 3,500 idle manzanas near León, the government proposed that the family keep part that would be good for dairy and give the rest to the state. But the family said they had no interest in the land. We offered them credit for dairy and guaranteed that if they wanted to develop it for dairy, we would never take it from them."

The law was passed last summer. How much land has been taken?

"Little. We are being very selective. We are concentrating where it is really possible to make an effective agrarian reform—where people are organized and have the capacity to use the land well. A good part of what we are officially redistributing was already de facto redistributed—where co-ops like the one you visited are already working idle lands. The law gives them legal status."

We know that your plans are not to increase the land in state farms and that you are actually redistributing some of the state farm land to cooperatives and to small farmer families. How has your view of the role of the state farm changed?

At this point Salvador smiled as if the point we had

raised was charged.

"In the ministry we have not changed our view of state farms. Of course the experience of the last few years affected us. But we never saw state farms as *the* answer. As for the direction we took in the beginning —turning abandoned Somoza land into state farms— we had no choice.

"But from the beginning we intended to promote cooperatives and we haven't changed. This is evident in the credit we've given to cooperatives and in how we've made land available rent-free to people organizing cooperatives.

"During the first two years we made significant steps in developing the state farms. Our efforts now and in the future are on organizing campesinos into cooperatives. We think that cooperatives ought to become the principal sector of agricultural development of the country. We hope that in 12, 15 or 20 years cooperatives might count for 50 percent of our production. The rest we see being divided more or less equally between the state farms and private producers —small, medium and large."

Do you think the campesinos share the ministry's enthusiasm for cooperatives? We thought that peasants were supposed to want only their own little plots?

"We have found real receptivity on the part of the peasants. Given our mistakes, everything would have collapsed if there hadn't been so much interest from the peasants! The very fact that we now have 2,500 cooperatives with about 60,000 people involved shows their enthusiasm. Of those 60,000 about 20 percent were wage laborers before, the rest tenants or sharecroppers."

What were your mistakes?

"For one, during the early period, we had to rely on donations of seeds from abroad. We gave the cooperatives seeds they were not accustomed to using. Some of the seeds didn't even germinate. And we gave out so much credit—in real terms a fivefold increase over what peasants ever got under Somoza. But we didn't always know what we were doing. We gave credit to cooperatives where there was not sufficient rainfall, where the land were not suitable. So some had big losses and big debts. Our overall policy of giving generous credit was good but we should have been more selective.

"Now we are trying to learn from these mistakes. We are trying to be more selective. Now we are in the process of choosing 150 cooperatives out of the 2,500. Some work the land together; others simply get their credit and technical assistance together. We will do everything we can to help them become strong so that they can have a demonstration effect."

What were the criteria used for the selection?

"Stability, commitment of the members to working together. We now have two years' track record to go on. Also we looked for economic potential."

What kind of help will these cooperatives receive?

"Help with marketing, technical problems, and bookkeeping. And we'll give them more land if they need it to operate efficiently. Some we hope to be able to help with irrigation. Of course, we will by no means neglect the other cooperatives. It's just a matter of focus, of making sure we do some fully right."

At that point we explained to Salvador that we also wanted to ask questions about his own life, about what path he took to be in this position now.

Tell us about your family, would you?

Salvador smiled as if knowing he was going to surprise us. "My family is, well, the traditional oligarchy. On my mother's side—the Sacasas—I am related to Somoza. But I have never cut off the ties with my family. Even when they were being punished by the Guard because of me and my brother, they never cut us off.

"My last year in high school is when it started. I was linked to the Christian student movement. We were very upset about the social situation in Nicaragua. The tradition in my family was to go to the U.S. to college. When I refused, there was a big conflict with my family. So I got together some friends who would go

Salvador Mayorga (left) officiating at ceremony granting land to cooperative

to the same university with me. We went to Rensselaer Polytechnic Institute in Troy, New York. This was 1971 and 1972. We tried to keep informed about what was happening in Nicaragua. And the Viet Nam war influenced us. We joined the movement against the war and even marched in some demonstrations in Boston.

"We knew that the peasant struggles were building up. We knew of the Sandinista Front; by that time it had a real political presence.

"Then I decided to transfer to Notre Dame where there were other Nicaraguans with social concerns. But eventually we decided to return to Nicaragua and enter the university here. I was in industrial engineering and involved in the Christian student movement again.

"Some of us went to live in a poor barrio in Managua with a Catholic priest. To support myself, and to learn how the majority of Nicaraguans lived, I worked as a bread vendor, earning only a few cordobas a day. There were eight or ten of us, all of whom are now in the government.

"We kept moving more and more on a political path. Somoza's corruption and brutality were more and more obvious. When the earthquake hit, I was living in a poor barrio. Living there, going through that experience with some of the poorest people in Managua, made an even clearer break with the tradition I grew up with.

"From there, the group I was living with took various paths. Some went to work with student groups, some stayed in the barrios and some went to fight with the guerrillas.

"I decided to work with peasants through the church and CEPA (See Justinian's interview on p. 49) and helped organize the first independent peasants' organization, the Association of Rural Workers (ATC). I helped develop their constitution."

What did your family think about your life?

"Remember I mentioned that they were threatened because of my work? About this time, 1978, the Guard broke into our house and threw my parents and my brother up against the wall. They really scared them. The Guard didn't really hurt anyone, though. If my family had been poor, they probably would have been killed.

"I know they suspected I was tied to the Front but they never cut me off. I think after this incident they had more sympathy for me, for what I was trying to do.

"During the final insurrection, I was in Diriamba. During those last few weeks, I became almost sure that we would win. So much was coming together at that point—the weakness of the National Guard, the unity of the Front, the determination of the people, and we had more arms."

At that point Salvador saw us react. He smiled and said:

"No, they weren't Soviet. I didn't see one single Soviet arm in the insurrection. I started the final insurrection with a French pistol. And the bullets they gave me weren't even the same caliber as the pistol!"

How did you end up here?

"Six days after victory, Jaime Wheelock (Minister of Agriculture) called. We had both worked together with the Association of Rural Workers (ATC) so he knew me. He asked me to work here."

It was after dark by then. Salvador looked tired and so we said good-bye. On the way out we peeked through the door to the adjoining room. It was a huge ornate bathroom with a large tub and gold gilded fixtures. Salvador smiled at our surprise. Another abandoned Somocista property called into public service.

Young volunteer brigadista for national literacy campaign

René Escoto

"A plastic kid"

At dinner that evening we met a young man who gave us further insight into the professional and personal changes that so many upper-class Nicaraguans are going through. René Escoto is a young researcher at the Institute for Economic and Social Research (INIES), a new nongovernmental center doing medium- and long-range planning for Central America and the Caribbean. René is white. While color differences are not often spoken about in Nicaragua, we learned that they correlate with differences in class background. René's white skin and delicate European features—not to mention his polo shirt—made us wonder if he were not from a well-to-do professional family. So we asked.

"Yes, the revolution has saved me from being what we call a 'plastic kid,' " he told us. "I could have easily been absorbed by U.S. culture—my head filled with American pop music (not that the music is so bad) or drugs or movies. In my head I would have been living in the United States, not in Nicaragua facing the realities of my people—which is uncomfortable."

Obviously you personally identify with the revolution. How do your parents react to this?

"Not well at all. We argue all the time at home. Sometimes they say that I must choose between them and the revolution. Since I love my parents, this has been very hard on me.

"From my early childhood, my parents have taught me to have upper-class, professional aspirations. In 1975 we moved from Matagalpa to Managua in part because they wanted me to go to the most prestigious private school in the country, the Jesuit school. Nothing has influenced me more than the Jesuits and, ironically, in the opposite direction of my parents' way of thinking. The Jesuits helped me examine my personal practice of Christianity, as a son, as a member of the school and in relations with others. The Jesuits encouraged me to participate in teaching literacy in the poor barrios of Managua, where for the first time I came into contact with the realities of the working people of my country.

"Following this, we students formed a group to live on Zapatera, an island in Lake Nicaragua. There also I saw how the campesinos lived, squeezed by a few large landowners. Every day we reflected on our experience in light of the Gospels. I became even more conscious of the system that impoverished so many in my country. We became aware that there was no way to help this island in the middle of the whole corrupt system without changing the system itself.

"Young people my age were being massacred in the working-class neighborhoods by Somoza's Guard. We began to realize that as Christians we could not be bystanders, we would have to fight against the biggest power, the real obstcle to a human life for most Nicaraguans. I worked hard to organize a movement of high school students, all from private religious schools. We were a little childish perhaps but it was our first try. Because we were from well-to-do families, we weren't persecuted by the Guardsmen. We weren't really afraid.

"But through this student organization we started to have contacts with public school students who were more revolutionary and more combative than we. Their courage to live underground really impressed me. We helped these revolutionary students with supplies, safe places for underground meetings, and money.

"The conflicts with our parents sharpened: some

of the kids in my school were sons of the highest National Guard officers. They sided with the Nicaraguan people and therefore opposed their parents, not as parents but because of their military position with the dictatorship. This really impressed me and provoked even more conflicts with my own parents.

"My parents were afraid that something would happen to me. My mother searched my room for pamphlets; when she found some, she became hysterical and threw them onto the patio to burn them. Then when the peak moment of the struggle against Somoza came and the Sandinistas called a national strike, my parents decided to take my brother and me out of Nicaragua and leave us with an uncle living in Los Angeles. At first I refused, but I was barely 15 years old. Finally I told them that I would go to the United States but it would be the last time I would give in to their will. I told them that when I returned after victory over Somoza (I knew it was close at hand), I would join in the work of the revolution despite any interference from them.

"So I went to the United States and spent June and early July 1979 with my uncle. I remember watching the television news constantly and seeing the big massacres. I saw young people murdered, good ordinary people assassinated in the barrios of Managua, the bombings by Somoza's air force, the National Guard's murder of the ABC newsman. All of this hurt me deeply. I kept asking myself: What am I, as a Christian, doing in the United States? My activity in the student organization had been phony because when the decisive moment came, I was not in Nicaragua but in another country looking after myself. From this pain was born a greater commitment to Nicaragua. I decided I would return to Nicaragua as soon as possible and throw myself into the work of the revolution."

What did you do when you returned to Nicaragua?

"First, we formed the Federation of High School Students, an organization for all the high schools, private and public, founded and directed by young people. And then I accepted an invitation to join the Sandinista Youth and began training volunteers for the literacy campaign. I was in charge of four squads, each with 30 student *brigadistas* (literacy teachers).

"Students from public and private schools were thrown together, but for once what distinguished us was not class but who worked harder, who merited more responsibility. This was a powerful experience with me: with my white skin and upper-class origin, I found that other students had expectations about me because of their own color and culture. But the literacy work brought us together.

"Politically I learned a lot by observing different attitudes of the *brigadistas* based on their backgrounds. For example, students from working-class families, from public schools, adapted to the living conditions quickly because they themselves had lived on the edge. But it was harder for them to learn how to teach. On the other hand, the *brigadistas* from well-off families and private schools were able to pick up the teaching techniques quickly—but it was harder for them to adapt to the new living conditions because they were used to more comfort."

What did your parents think about your participation in the literacy campaign?

"My parents put unrelenting pressure on me to quit. They sometimes visited me and couldn't understand why their son was living in such poor conditions. They were dead set against my being in the Sandinista Youth. They said the literacy campaign was communism, that we were brainwashing the campesinos, that my god was the government, that the government was robbing parents of their sons and daughters. They didn't understand that we were trying to eliminate the enormous injustices with which we were living. They didn't understand that the first step, the one in which all the young people of Nicaragua were involved, was literacy.

"They couldn't see the overall thrust of the revolution—they just fixated on some errors committed by the government. So this conflict with my parents was the principal problem for me during the campaign. It was very tough for me. Especially on birthdays—mine, my father's, my mother's—when they insisted that I come to Managua. But that was out of the question for me, especially, since, as the person in charge of so many *brigadistas*, I had to set a good example and not go back to Managua for this or that. Imagine if all the *brigadistas* had traveled home to Managua for all these birthdays! It would have meant enormous expenditures.

"Through the literacy campaign my Christian faith deepened. I came to understand the Christian commitment much better, what the Latin American bishops in Puebla called 'the preferential option for the poor.' I began to really identify with the Gospel, with all the words that sometimes seem so abstract, so up in the clouds, so romantic when you just read them in the Bible. I came to understand these words concretely when I was living in poverty with the campesinos, when I was teaching them to read and write, and learning how they live and all the things they experience in the countryside. Then I could understand, if I opened my eyes a little, all that the Scriptures teach."

What did you do after the campaign finished?

"I went back home—to the same conflicts with my parents. They put tremendous pressure on me to quit the Sandinista Youth. Finally I decided to obey them

until I finished high school so that they couldn't say I had been brainwashed or that someone was taking their son away. I felt very bad about myself, but it was a necessary step with my parents. During this entire time I dedicated myself to my studies to avoid ideological confrontations with my parents. They had to see that even though for a whole year and a half I was not being "brainwashed" by the Sandinista Youth I still had the same commitment to the revolution.

"Once I graduated from high school, I decided to enter the university, rejoin the Sandinista Youth, and again work in the revolution. My parents objected, but now I had a job working here at the Institute, and I attended university classes so I was at home very little."

What are your plans now?

"I've just made a difficult decision. Late last year I was offered a scholarship by the British government to study economics at the university in Sussex. At first I rejected it outright because I thought I couldn't be taken away from the revolution—I just couldn't miss out on all the experiences. I talked the scholarship over with some of the social scientists here at the Institute and with some Jesuits, trying to analyze the situation of young people and the future of the revolution.

"The lack of committed professionals is one of the weaknesses of this revolution. This revolution is strong in its popular base and strong militarily—not because we have a lot of weapons, because they are pitiful when compared to the armaments of other countries, but simply because all of us are ready to fight, to die, to defend our country. So after much talking and reflection with others, I decided to accept the scholarship. In England I hope to synthesize what is good for creative uses in the Nicaraguan reality. I'm not going to get wrapped up in the social traditions there, especially Anglo-Saxon individualism. My greatest desire is to come back here and work during the summer vacations to keep in close touch with the situation in my country."

Are your parents pleased?

"Their reaction has been mixed. They know my deep commitment to the revolution. At the same time I think they are happy to see me out of Nicaragua. Like so many in their privileged class, they're moving to Miami where they've been fattening their bank account for many years."

From everything you say it is clear that your fundamental motivations are Christian. Does Marxism conflict with your faith?

"I really don't feel any problem. My faith motivates me to build the kingdom of God *here*, as we say in the Lord's Prayer. And what are the things that keep this kingdom of God from existing here on earth, here in

Nicaragua? A series of injustices, economic, social, political, which are wrapped up in a capitalist system that Nicaragua has experienced, a bourgeoisie that didn't give a damn how the rest of the people lived and a military dictatorship that maintained this deeply unjust system and beat back every rebellion by the campesinos and workers.

"Thus it is my faith, the Gospel, that compels me to commit myself politically to Nicaragua. I commit myself to carry out the work that can bring about for the first time an economic, social, and political context that will allow those who have traditionally been exploited and repressed to go on liberating themselves. I don't see any contradiction with Marxism. On the contrary, I see it as a tool of analysis for helping to change our society, a tool that has to be adapted to the practice in specific situations. Moreover, in Nicaragua today I don't believe in anyone simply because they expound this or that philosophy. I look at what he or she is doing. The person who shows revolutionary practice in all the tasks of the revolution, the popular health workshops, the militia, adult education, the CDS, work, and school, that's the only person who has the right to say that his or her ideology is the correct one. And those like my parents who cry "Atheism, atheism" —they don't impress me at all, because Somoza said he believed in God yet he killed and killed."

Ciudad Sandino: Life in the Barrio

The Maryknoll sisters had invited us to visit their home in Ciudad Sandino, a large, poor barrio on the outskirts of Managua. We left a little early the next morning so we would have time to stop and look around before arriving there.

As we entered the barrio, the most striking structure was the market that the government had recently built. Before, the barrio's 70,000 residents had to travel ten miles into Managua to shop or sell their goods at the old *Mercado Oriental*, or Eastern Market.

We walked into the first of the structures—large, sturdy, and brightly painted sheds, each housing a dozen or so stalls for the vendors of food and other basic items. We stopped at the very first stall and

Angela

introduced ourselves.

We met Angela Gomez, a friendly, soft-spoken woman in her thirties and her young children who gathered around with curiosity as we spoke.

Our obvious first question: what do you think of the new market?

"Well, I don't have to get up at 4 a.m. anymore to take the bus to Managua. Now I can sleep until 6. It's cleaner here, it's more organized and since I live here my children can come here with me."

What about prices? Are you selling your products any cheaper here?

"I sell at lower prices now. But I make about the same because I get a lot of the food at lower, controlled prices from the government. When their prices are cheaper, I get some products from the private wholesalers instead of the government. Whichever is cheaper."

Some people are against these new markets and want to keep the old Oriental. The government says it is inefficient to have people traveling long distances to go to one central market. They want people to use the new ones, near to where they live. What do you think?

"They came here and took a census of all the people who live here and sell in the Oriental. They asked us who would like to sell here in the new market. I don't know the results of the census but I do know that most of the people who were selling in the Oriental are still there."

But why, if this is so much more convenient?

"They're afraid of going bankrupt. I guess they have their clients there and are afraid of losing them if they move. But it's just an idea in their heads. Look at me. I started here with nothing. I didn't fail. I'm doing well.

"It's true a couple of people have gone out of business, but it was because they didn't have enough products. Also, they were already in debt and the bank wouldn't give them more.

How did you get started?

"The government gave me credit at 7 percent interest. They offered that to all of us. A moneylender would charge 20 percent!"

How else has the revolution affected you?

"The biggest change of course is the government. But you don't feel that much day to day. Poor working people continue working—as always. You have to be realistic about that!

"But there is a big improvement in the neighborhood. Before victory, we had no street lights, we had no market and we had no paved roads."

What do you think of the CDS neighborhood organizations? Are you involved?

"Yes, I'm the one responsible for the CDS in this building. Each of the buildings in the market has its own CDS. Our main work is to keep watch to see to it that some people don't raise prices. There have been some conflicts about this. A 25-centavo price change doesn't seem like much. But it can affect someone's pocketbook."

What do you think of the government's plan to shut the Oriental?

"That would be very bad. There wouldn't be enough

places in other markets for everyone. Some would be excluded."

As we were thanking her, we flashed back to the first marketwoman we had met, who was full of hostility toward the government. Such a contrast to Angela. Angela, too, had criticisms, but she was actively involved and could see the positive changes in her life. Why such contrasts? Both women had the same jobs and probably similar opportunities, yet their reactions were entirely different.

One woman, with a vested interest in the stall she had, was afraid of change (even though it might have helped her). She just wanted to be left alone. The other saw an opportunity she had never had, thus she welcomed change. She was critical yet supportive.

Such differences exist within every society. In most, those afraid of change predominate; in a society trying to transform itself, those ready to embrace change become the leaders. A critical test for Nicaragua will be how well it, as a society in transition, copes with personalities afraid of change.

"Back to the sixth grade—are you kidding?"

We couldn't find the Maryknoll sisters' house so we stopped and asked a couple of kids on the street. They knew.

Entering their bungalow, we saw on the walls a

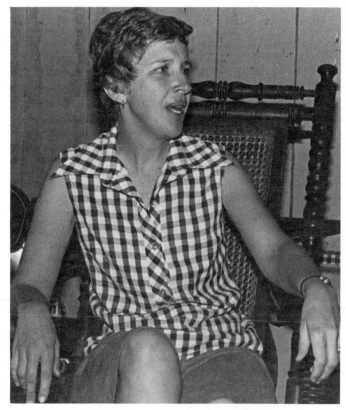

Julianne Warnshuis

prominent poster of the sisters killed last year in El Salvador for doing precisely the work among the poor that Pat Edmiston and Julianne Warnshuis have done for years in Nicaragua. (One of the assassinated sisters, Maura Clark, had worked in Ciudad Sandino during part of her more than 20 years in Nicaragua.) Sipping tea in the side yard adjoining their modest house, we first asked about the dispute over the government's plan to open new marketplaces throughout the city and close down the huge Oriental.

"What the government is proposing is hardly radical," Pat said. "Before the earthquake, there were five markets spread throughout the city. Just one big market for all Managua is relatively recent—what the government proposes is returning to the old system. The government says that the Oriental is horribly unsanitary and dominated by price-gouging wholesalers."

Both Pat and Julianne are Americans, so we talked of how the Sandinista government is viewed back home. We told them that Americans are told that Nicaragua is a totalitarian, repressive society. In responding, they tried to help us get a feeling for the situation in Nicaragua.

"You have to understand what revolution does to people," Juilianne told us. "For the first time people are not afraid. They have been taking orders all their lives. Now they feel they're not going to accept orders from anyone!

"This was especially true for young people. They were the raw power behind the victory. But with victory, many of them were lost. They had won! No one was going to tell them what to do. Most young kids over 14 had experienced carrying and using arms. 'I'm not going back to sit in sixth grade. Are you kidding?' You couldn't keep the kids in school. They were climbing the walls. They'd lived in the dark so long. Suddenly the lights were on. There was a psychological eruption.

"The government wanted to take that energy and start building with it, but how? The Sandinista leadership saw literacy as an essential element in the process of the Nicaraguan revolution. They wanted to implement a literacy campaign right away, even though many advised them not to try yet. 'It is much too soon,' they were warned by many experts. Nevertheless, they started organizing the literacy campaign only one month after victory. It was an opportunity to achieve simultaneously many objectives of the revolution. While the urban schooled youth could give of their knowledge, at the same time they benefitted from the experience of seeing and living in other parts of the country, especially getting to know the reality of the campesinos, their life and work. Moreover, these young people were disciplined and they understood the big task expected of them. It was a big success all around."

Sister Pat added, "Outsiders look at the literacy campaign and are put off by the military rhetoric and discipline. But both were necessary to give the kids boundaries and a sense of direction. And now some people look at the militia and think that the government is trying to develop a military mentality. But with threats coming from the ex-Guardsmen, the Honduran Army, and their U.S. backers, they can't let down. It's not military mentality here. It's the attitude that 'if we have to defend ourselves, yes we will. But in the meantime we'll go about our ordinary lives.' "

Julianne picked up on Pat's point: "The military is not a separate force like under Somoza. The soldiers are not arrogant and apart from the people. Under Somoza, you never would see a member of the Guard get on a bus or help an old person cross a crowded highway. There was a complete separation. Now the military and the police are just like other people. And no one's afraid to talk back to them."

Because Sister Pat is a nurse, we then turned the conversation to her experiences working on health care in the barrio.

What difference do you see today compared to the health conditions under Somoza?

"First of all, keep in mind that more than 70,000 people live in this barrio. For all these people, we had one clinic and one doctor and one nurse. And they worked only three to four hours a day. And only on weekdays!

"Now we have three clinics and ten doctors. In all, we have 70 medical personnel. We have a well-baby clinic and a center for pregnant women. Five health promoters circulate throughout the barrio helping people get latrines and clean up debris that might breed insects.

"Since the victory, all medicine has been free. But that is being changed now because the richer people were taking advantage of the system. The clinic charges one cordoba—ten cents—per consultation. This isn't a standard rule of the Ministry of Health. Our CDS started it so that we would have a fund to buy items the clinic needs."

What about malnutrition?

"Yes, there is some malnutrition—very little third degree; some second and a lot of first degree. But what I notice here in the barrio is that, before, almost every day a little coffin would come by in a funeral procession. Now you don't see that.

"In the country as a whole infant mortality has been reduced from the extremely high 120 per 100,000 to 94. This is not great, but it's a significant change.

"Many children were dying of childhood diseases, made much worse because hunger weakened their bodies. I saw so many little children die of hemorrhagic measles, the most horrible disease you can imagine. Blood starts coming out of all of the orifices. But in 1979, with the help of the block organizations, the government carried out a vaccination campaign against measles. Now we see very few cases.

"This year was to be the Year of Health. But because of the threats against the country, the government had to change it to the Year of Production and Defense. But still, there's been an emphasis on popular health campaigns.

"Since last March we've had four vaccination campaigns—for malaria, for measles, for diphtheria and last Sunday for polio. It was 90 percent successful. Can you imagine how much work it took to achieve that? And almost all volunteer labor. There was the census to find out how many vaccines were needed, setting up the stations, distributing the vaccine (and getting the ice for it in this climate!), administering it and keeping the records. Without the support of the people, this just could not have been done."

Pat continued with a reflection on her recent trip back home to visit her family in Yonkers.

"I saw a TV spot on the mayor of some place back in New Jersey out in the park picking up litter. The message was community self-help—great! Well, that's what is happening here, but Americans can't see it.

This is a poor country. What else is going to help them? That's all they have.

"What I've seen here *is* grassroots democracy. People figuring out their own solutions. There's a barrio committee to help people with problems. Nobody could afford to be at the office fulltime so the nine-member secretariat elected one person to be full-time and paid. That person is paid by the national CDS from the dues (2 cordobas per week) that each member of the local CDS pays."

But how do you respond to criticism that the CDSs are really just tools for those in control to oversee other people's lives? And that those who are active in the CDSs get special privileges?

"Well, I can't say it doesn't happen but I haven't seen it work that way. But if there are more and more terrorist attacks, there will probably be more and more vigilance.

"Beginning, I think, in 1980, everyone must have a letter—a *constancia*—from the CDS identifying them."

But why? Could this be used against people?

"Let me give you an example of one of the reasons it is needed. Health care is divided up by zone and people are expected to go to the doctor in their zone, otherwise we can't care for everyone. The problem is that some doctors are more popular. There is one Cuban doctor that everyone loves. So people try to give a false address to get to see him and other doctors they like. The letter from the CDS makes it harder for people to do this.

"The CDS is not allowed to write anything bad about a person on the letter, although people really active in the CDS might have this mentioned in theirs."

But couldn't that in itself lead to abuse? To these people getting special favors? Or to people who didn't have this kind of note being discriminated against? It is this kind of surveillance function that some people fear in the CDS model.

"Yes, I can't say it couldn't go that way. But it's not that way now. If the counterrevolutionaries start to sabotage, it *could* happen.

"Let me give you an example of one function of the CDS that outsiders might look at and cry 'repression!' But they wouldn't know what they are talking about.

"If you want to have a party, you have to have the permission of the CDS on your block."

Our eyes widened. My God, we thought, how is she going to defend this? How would we like it if we had to go around and ask our neighbors if we could throw a party?

"This decision came out of a lot of grassroots discussion. People themselves see that the abuse of alcohol is a tremendous problem in Nicaragua. Nicaraguans are very peaceful people—except when they're

Pat Edmiston

drunk. Then they can be very violent. Fights, knifings, even shootings were not uncommon on a Saturday night.

"Understand, too, that a party here is different than at home. Often it's a business where people sell drinks."

So how does getting permission from the block group help?

"Well, remember it's all the people who know you who give permission. So you know that if your party gets out of control, you may not get permission next time. When you have to get permission, you take it more seriously. You have to have one person there who is responsible at all times. If something bad happens, that person is in charge.

"This system may seem strange to us. But it is a decision of the neighborhood, of people trying to work out their own problems."

"To prevent speculation..."

Leaving Ciudad Sandino, we stopped at a *tienda popular*, one of the food outlets established by the government offering people in the poor barrios the basics at controlled prices.

The first thing we noticed as we approached the checkout counter was that in the spot usually loaded with "impulse items" such as candy, gum and magazines, we saw paperback poetry!

We introduced ourselves to the proprietor and asked him what purpose he saw these stores serving.

"They prevent speculation. I've been here two years and I can see the difference. We don't allow people to buy in large quantities and hoard any more.

"There used to be lines for sugar. Whenever there was a scare of sugar shortage, people would send four members of their family four times a day to buy sugar. Now we limit people to one pound per person per week. There are no lines."

Looking around we saw not only the basic foods but lots of other items including liquor and even Kellogg's corn flakes.

"We used to sell just 37 basic items but now we handle many more. So gradually more people are coming here. It's a question of time. People are beginning to see that things cost more in the other stores."

Walking through the store, we were struck by the signs and messages on some of the packaging, exhorting people to be frugal. "The good revolutionary consumes only what is necessary," said one government message referring to sugar.

The contrast between this well-stocked *tienda popular* (people's store) and the sparsely stocked one we visited near Santa Maria was striking. What we learned in Santa Maria is that many people did not take advantage of the cheaper prices for basic goods because the store didn't have enough variety of other goods to make their trip pay. Here near the capital city, this problem appeared more solvable.

Demonstration of workers supporting donation of 13 month salary to the unemployed

What is a Labor Union in New Nicaragua?

Before noon we arrived at the national headquarters of the ATC, the farmworkers' association affiliated with the Sandinistas. There we were also to meet a representative of UNAG, the union of small farmers and ranchers.

Like just about all the topics we were pursuing in Nicaragua, the role of unions is controversial. Opponents of the government see the progovernment unions as tools of the government; defenders see them playing a critical role in trying to protect the interests of the workers within the limits of what is possible, given the country's poverty.

We knew that we wouldn't be able to resolve the question in this interview. But we could find out how

Germán Benavides

the association officials themselves view their role.

Germán Benavides, an official of the ATC, is the son of a tailor and a laundress. His awareness of the plight of farmworkers began when, as a young teenager, he picked cotton during summer vacations. In 1976, as a student in a technical school, Germán made contact with the revolutionary student movement.

What were your motives?

"I lived the poverty of the majority of Nicaraguans.

Many times I had no money for food, for clothing, or books. Once I linked up with the student movement, I began to understand some of the causes of our poverty.

"The history they taught us in school was very distorted. It never spoke of our true history—of the peasants being pushed off the land by the rich landowners who wanted to grow cotton, coffee, and sugar. The history we learned all favored the dictatorship.

"I left school and was in the first insurrection in Chinandega. Fleeing from the Guard into Honduras I was captured by the Honduran army who later moved us to Costa Rica, because of pressure on Honduras from Somoza. From Costa Rica I got back into the country and took part in the final insurrection."

How did the association get started?

"In 1976 the political organizers for the Sandinista Front began setting up committees of farmworkers, especially on the coffee estates.

"We worked by targeting key haciendas just before harvest time. At harvest we knew we'd have the most leverage in gaining concessions from the landowners. We worked intensively with the farmworkers, explaining the meaning of the Somoza regime, the situation of poverty and the role they had to play to change things. We pressed for better housing conditions, food, wages, and treatment by the manager.

"After harvest, when many workers returned home, we went into their villages so as not to lose the organizational impetus. We would work on things close to the people—improving the roads, schools and things like that.

"Of course, we also introduced political awareness into our work so that people would see the necessity of overthrowing Somoza.

"Then, in March 1978, we had the first national assembly and the ATC was officially constituted. At this assembly we approved setting up military training centers for campesino cadres who would work against Somoza—helping columns get through the countryside, sabotaging production, interrupting roads.

"The association also had an important role in the liberated areas. We planted basic foods so the people wouldn't go hungry. This brought us very close to the people.

"At the time of triumph, the association was a force of 12,000 men and women. Now, two and a half years later, we have 80,000 members. there are 1,250 locals of the Farmworkers Association on both private and state farms.

Before UNAF was created we had 120,000 members. The small farmers and ranchers split off to form UNAG because their interests are different from those of landless farmworkers."

" . . . *so the workers don't just operate as machines*"

What are the goals of the association now?

"We're fighting for three things—to participate in management, to organize a militia, and to carry out adult education on each of the farms.

"Adult education is vitally important so that our workers can become more technically skilled. How can you talk about participation in management if the workers are unskilled?

"We've formed study circles to help the workers understand the economic model of the new society and what are the benefits to them. All this is so that the workers don't just operate as machines.

"It's difficult work. The technicians on the farms were educated in Somoza's universities. They were brought up with a style of work that we want to change through greater participation by the workers. The revolution lacks suffcent technicians so we have to work with these people and bring them along."

What is the difference in the kind of work you do on the state farms compared to the private farms?

"The difference between the state and the private is that on the state farms the doors are open to change. On the private farms we are mostly looking out for decapitalization. But we have also set up militias and adult education circles.

"It's easier to work on the state farms, so there's a tendency to give more of our energy there. We're really forcing ourselves to have more of a presence on the private farms. We want to make sure that production is maintained and that the government credits are used well. Part of our battle is to get the information we need about production on the private farms."

Do you find a lot of decapitalization by farm owners who are against the revolution?

"Most of the large owners are letting their farms and machinery run down, trying to get their money out and certainly underproducing. But the small and medium farm owners are carrying out a patriotic role, producing as best they can."

" . . . *The tortilla has been turned*"

Critics of Nicaragua would say that the Farmworkers Association is just a political organization supporting the government and therefore can't really represent the interests of the workers.

"Every union in Nicaragua has a political orientation. Ours is the Front. Every organization is either for the government or against it. We consider that the Sandinista government is a popular government that represents and defends our interests. The Somoza government only defended the interests of a small group of men and women who killed and tortured. Now the tortilla has been turned.

"We know that your government is attacking us. But we believe that each country should be allowed the freedom to work out its own destiny. We also know that the U.S. government doesn't represent the interests of the U.S. people themselves."

What about the unions who don't support the government? What is their role?

"There is great division within the labor movement. And in workplaces where there is conflict between two unions, the disputes can have repercussions in production. Given the state of our economy, this is very serious. So we have tried to solve this through a coordinating group where the union representatives can talk with each other."

What is the difference in approach between your union and one not supporting the government?

"Well, take the CTN, the Nicaraguan Labor Federation. At the state owned sugar mill Xavier Guerra, the CTN encouraged workers to sabotage machines and strike. If the workers feel they are hungry, the CTN seizes on this to tell the workers that the 'revolution' is a demogogic word. They try to turn the workers against the government instead of helping them to understand the objective problems, instead of trying

to help them to understand that political will is not enough—it will take time and hard work to change the objective conditions of poverty.

"Because of threats against our country, people hoard goods in order to sell them later if things get worse. This creates scarcity. If everything were properly distributed, there would be no scarcity. This type of issue is manipulated by some of the unions. It is completely against the interests of the country."

" . . . guaranteed the right of private property"

The conversation turned next to focus on the problems of small farmers and ranchers. Hermogenes Rodriguez is a member of the national governing body of UNAG, the association of small farmers and ranchers which split off from the Farmworkers Association in 1980. Hermogenes also represents UNAG on the Council of State.

"I didn't fight with the Sandinistas like Germán. From about 1970 onward, though, I worked clandestinely to support the Front. For a long time the Front tried to think of ways to dialogue with Somoza. But the repression was so great they had to go underground.

"I worked with small and medium farmers. They participated in the struggle, supplying and even joining the Front. They helped with medicine, food, as couriers of information. Through the entire sector, from the very first years. So they recognize the role that the Front has played. They knew Somoza was selling us out.

"Now what we see has happened is a change from a regime of hate to a regime where people have rights, have freedom within the framework of a mixed economy which guarantees private property.

"Even while the war was still going on, the Front promised and guaranteed the right of private property."

What is your own background?

"My family owns 200 manzanas (350 acres) and produces coffee and cattle in Jinotega. I would study for eight months of the year and work four months on the farm. This is what the government now says it hopes more young people will do.

"Somoza didn't permit the small or medium producer to have any real surplus. The surplus went to the large landowners and to the middlemen. There was no surplus that would allow people like my father to develop their farms.

"This work with my family's farm helps me be very clear in my own mind. It helps me to translate the Sandinista vision."

What does your family think of your work? Do they support the government too?

"My father is dead. The rest of my family is in agreement. They understand because they have experienced it personally. What they want is what the government is now doing. They want democracy and a mixed economy. This is what the Sandinistas promised us and we haven't been betrayed."

"Private production is a way of supporting the revolution"

Who are your members and what are their interests?

"Right now we have 40,000 members, or about 20 percent of all the small and medium producers. Some have been pushed off their land and are struggling to regain it. Others are small farmers whose land is not adequate—maybe the soil is too poor or they have too little. Still others are medium producers who are in debt and don't have the tools, irrigation, and other things that they need. We're trying to help them all.

"You don't have to be a Sandinista to be a member of UNAG, but you do have to be in basic agreement with the revolutionary process. And you have to support the revolution by producing. We show people that genuine private production—including more profits—is a way of supporting the revolutionary process.

"We've had to clarify for people that the revolution is not communism. Anticommunist propaganda has really held this sector back from developing."

How is UNAG structured?

"We are democratic and elective. At every level of the organization, governing *juntas* are elected.

"We've felt a lot of euphoria this year about getting organized. We're doing a lot of work with people, not just blindly signing them up. We don't want a million members if they don't understand what UNAG is.

"Because of their organizing work some of our members have been killed by counterrevolutionaries.

"Part of what is new is having a seat in the Council of the State. Under Somoza, small farmers like us were cut off from government services—credit, technical advice, etc. Under Somoza, the big boys, the rich landowners, said they spoke for us. We had no voice.

"In November, 1980, representatives of the big growers left the Council of State, announcing that the entire farming sector was leaving! But *we*, the small and medium producers, are the overwhelming majority. They gave the world the very wrong impression that the entire productive sector was against the revolution."

"Cooperatives are the road to progress"

What is UNAG's role in helping cooperatives?

"We are encouraging people to join cooperatives because of the services they offer. Of course, it's volun-tary. At the time of triumph, there was a general fear of cooperatives. Somoza used to say that cooperatives were the road to communism. We tell people that cooperatives are the road to progress.

"Now people are changing. They are changing because they can see how the cooperatives are working and improving people's lives. We try to help clarify the issues for people. And we see the support for cooperatives growing tremendously.

"Our goal for 1982 is to help to consolidate 300 new cooperatives. More than half of them cooperate mainly for credit and technical assistance; the others involve some form of shared work too."

We returned to the same challenge we had presented to Germán: Critics of the Nicaragua system would say that your union is just a tool of the government and therefore not truly able to serve the interests of your members.

"We are not a state organization or a parastatal organization. We're a private, patriotic organization. We get no financing from the state. Our budget comes from the fees of our membership. But we support the revolutionary process. We supported it during the clandestine period and we continue to.

"We created UNAG to make sure that the government does not deviate from what it said it would do. We want genuine democracy, not bourgeois democracy where just a few people are involved. We're working for that democracy by supporting the needs of our members. We help to carry out services which the government wants to supply to small farmers."

Husking corn, Coyolito farm cooperative near Esteli

"People just turn up every day"

The next day we drove south to visit a cooperative to find out how the members themselves think cooperatives are working. But, on the way, we stopped at the home of two development workers (he Swiss, she Canadian) and their young twin boys.

Sitting on the porch enjoying a freshly baked pineapple upside down cake and "coffee" made from roasted, ground beans, they told us that after years of experience they had decided not to work through official aid agencies any more. "We can be much more effective on our own," they told us.

They went on to explain how their work in Nicaragua contrasts with their experience of the other Central American countries.

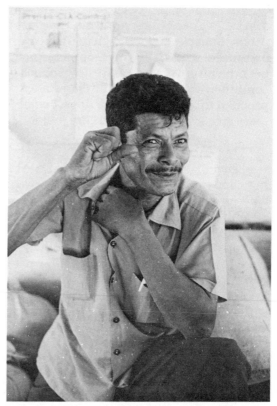

Asunción

"In Guatemala," the Swiss, Curt Rhyner Pozak, told us, "we used to spend all our time just trying to get people to participate. But here the people are already organized, so I can use my technical knowledge. We've been helping villages build new schools—helping to come up with better building materials. And there's no problem in getting the work done. People just turn up every day. It's all voluntary. They just join in."

"... *Waiting for the animal to die*"

Leaving our friends, we soon reached the farming cooperative, which had just received title to its land after a year-long struggle. This cooperative was on land which had been part of the giant Pastora farm, a 24,000-acre estate of which all but 85 acres was left uncultivated by the owner. (See our book, *What Difference Can a Revolution Make?*) After petitioning the government to take over some of the idle land and give it to their cooperative, a group of poor peasants had simply taken the land and begun planting the food crops they needed.

It was almost noon when we arrived. The sun was bright as the wind whipped through the trees. Driving up to the main building, we were met by Asunción, the main organizer of the cooperative, and several other members including a woman and her young teenage daughters. For the next few hours we talked, sitting on their sacks of recently harvested corn and beans—their proof that "we won't be hungry any more," as Asunción told us.

We began asking Asunción about his family's history. His story is all too typical of the how the poor in most countries lose their land to those with money and therefore political connections.

"About thirty years ago we went to live with my father in the hills. We worked and worked and worked and finally got enough money to buy 120 manzanas. We had enough to feed ourselves then. But someone with connections at the bank came and burned our crop, leaving us with a huge debt. The bank started threatening to take our land. My father went to the Ministry of Land Titles and Taes and tried to explain and asked for more time. They said we had 48 hours to pay. They knew we couldn't. The rich people were just hovering like vultures waiting for the animal to die.

"To pay our debts we ended up having to sell our land for 18,000 cordobas. That was in 1964. The man who bought it sold it the very next year for 36,000 cordobas. In that one deal he made more money than we make in several years of work.

"After we lost our land we moved here and started renting land from the same owner who had thrown us off our land. But we couldn't get enough land to make it through the year. We had to work as wage laborers for the *patron*, too. He really had us by the throat. He wanted to turn us into *colonos*, by denying us enough land to survive on.

"Being a *colono* is like being a slave. You don't have any land except the little plot around your house. You work on it til 2:00 and then do a thousand jobs for the owner. He gives you some food and clothes and then takes it out of your pay. So at the end of the year you could even owe the *patron!*

"And all the *patrones* were interested in is products for export—cattle, coffee, or, in other places, sugar."

When did you start working toward the cooperative here?

"Things began to change in 1972. That was the year a Colombian came and helped us get organized. Before we were blind, sleeping. But he taught us that if we got organized, we could get land. Twenty-two of us got together and pressured the government for land. We got it—but we were still renting. We worked for three years. All the dispossessed people wanted to join us.

"At that time the cooperative just meant getting together to have more power to get the credit to get the land, not working the land together like we do now.

"But in late 1974, the National Guard came in and beat us up and kicked us off the land. The Guard attacked us as part of the persecution against Father Gaspar."

"I began to understand human rights..."

Who was this Father Gaspar?

"He was one of the priests in this area who helped us to understand the Bible and human rights for the first time.

"Before I couldn't understand. It was like the priests spoke a foreign language. But when Father Gaspar and some of the other priests came, they began to speak in a language I could understand.

"I began to understand what human rights are all about. There are no limits on what human beings can do once you understand what human rights are all about.

"God made all that we see around us—the trees and the mountains. But God is invisible. If the world was made by Him, but He is not visible, not here, that means the world belongs to all of us.

"Human rights means the right to food, to land.

"I began to think about this a lot. I began to see that the world could be a kingdom of love and not hate. The kingdom of love is what is most interesting to us. You are from North America; yet we are brothers. We have one Father.

"I wasn't the only one to wake up. There were a lot

of us who began to realize these things. There were a lot of people who helped us. I became a Delegate of the Word in 1972 and Felipe, here in 1974. We worked with CEPA (See Justinian interview on page 49) and the Association of Rural Workers (ATC). (See pages 28 and 97).

"Of course, all of this had to be clandestine. But the National Guard really began to persecute us. During mass, a Guardsman would stand at the doorway of each church to make sure that nothing happened and to listen to what the priest said.

"There were many people involved in the struggle, in working for better health and education and all. But when the moment of truth came , only 36 of us went with Father Gaspar to fight with the Sandinistas. That was January 27, 1978." (Father Gaspar was assassinated on December 11, 1978.)

But what about this land you have now. Who did it belong to and how did you get it?

"This land was owned by the Pastora family. Pastora was a conservative and in 1911 when the Conservative candidate won the presidency, he told his generals—yes you can have that land, go and take it. Pastora was one of them. Now this farm goes from here all the way down to San Juan del Sur (about ten miles). This part right here used to belong to the village—it had been common land used for foraging cattle.

Pastora got the mayor to turn it over to him.

"After our victory, I came back from the mountains and one of my goals was to really get us organized, to really know where are headed. I've been working here ever since and it's getting better every day.

"His cattle would die of hunger"

"We could see that almost none of the Pastora land was planted—maybe 50 manzanas out of 14,000. So first we went to the ATC to get their help in getting some of this unused land.

"The association told us that first we should go to Pastora and ask him if we could rent the land. They said that if he said no, we could take the land we need and the association would support us. So we went to talk personally with Pastora. He said no. He told us that he had his cattle to worry about and that if he let us rent some land, his cattle would die of hunger.

"So 16 of us sharpened up our machetes and came in here and started getting the land ready for planting. Pastora sent his overseer out to tell us to get off, that we had no right to the land. We said, 'We are going to keep working this land. No one is going to push us off.'

"When the overseer told Pastora what was happening, Pastora went to the ATC headquarters in Tola and complained. The association told him, 'The land can't be idle anymore. People are dying of hunger.' They told

Pastora that the only thing he could do was make a deal with us."

Asunción continued his story in detail, telling us how at first Pastora conceded, allowing them to rent 27 acres. But when the group grew and needed more land, he kept resisting, insisting that "my cattle just can't withstand this." The first year, the group had planted 79 acres.

"We went to Pastora at the end of the season to pay the rent. We told him: 'you can eat off us and we'll eat off the land. But this year we need 100 manzanas.' Remember, he had 14,000. But Pastora said, 'absolutely not.'

"It was after this that we started organizing demonstrations to get the government behind us. We wanted the government to confiscate the land because our people are dying of hunger and have no place to live or work. We had been through the legal procedures —trying to get him to rent. This had failed.

"Our first demonstration was right here in Tola. The Farmworkers' Association helped us organize it. Nearly 300 people showed up. Then we turned out 500 people for a demonstration in front of the Ministry of Agriculture headquarters in Rivas (a bigger nearby town). We asked the ministry for vehicles to take our people to Managua to talk with the head of the agrarian reform—that is Salvador Mayorga. Some of us had worked with him during the struggle. We trusted him.

"As soon as Salvador came out of his office and saw me, he knew who I was. 'What are you people asking for?' he asked. And 600 people entered his offices. So many people came because they had hope for themselves for the first time. Some saw a chance to stop being *colonos* and have land of their own. They saw us as people who could get things done and they got stirred up.

"When we explained everything we had done, Salvador agreed with us. He declared a confiscation of the Pastora farm that very day.

"Of course, in *La Prensa* Pastora attacked the government as a bunch of bloodthirsty communists and started a legal suit which went to the Supreme Court. It ruled that the land should go back to Pastora. But while all this was going on, the legal basis for taking over the land was being laid by the new agrarian reform law, passed last summer. Once it was passed, there was no question. It guaranteed us the land. And on December 11, 1981 we got legal title."

"The revolution is generous . . . "

Asunción's victory in the battle for the right to land doesn't mean that he fully supports what the government is doing now.

"The ministry is making a big mistake now in

dividing up the land into individual parcels. They should only give it to cooperatives," he told us.

"Even some of the cooperatives are really reactionary. They are being manipulated by the big landowners here. The landowners are telling these cooperatives that the people in the other cooperatives—that's us—are communists. They warn them: 'Be careful, the state is going to come back and take the land away from you again.' One of these big owners has two farms. He's against the government because one of his farms is idle—and he's afraid the agrarian reform will take his idle land.

"I have a lot of arguments with the people in the Ministry of Agricultural Development. Why give the parcels to individuals? They answer that 'the revolution is generous. We have to help people even if they don't want to be in cooperatives.' "

Obviously Asunción clearly believed that cooperatives offer peasants the best hope for development. This in itself intrigued us. So we pushed Asunción to explain.

"Well, you are more motivated when you work together. We could never have achieved what we have here by working alone. We could never even have gotten the land. But there a lot of advantages. If I get sick, for example, the others can continue my work so we don't lose the crop. Also, by myself some of the physical work would be so much harder. And there are things a cooperative can do that an individual just can't. By having more resources, the cooperative can get more credit and new technology. And it makes more sense for the government to send the technicians to help a group than to help people one by one."

But don't some work harder than others? Aren't there lazy ones who make the others work for them?

"Sure, some people have more strength than others. Some are more motivated. That does create tension. But we talk about these things. We work it out."

"... *peace but not peace with hunger*"

It was clear that for Asunción, the struggle was not over. In fact it was just beginning. He is the president of the local UNAG, but he suggested that his views are quite controversial.

"If we don't expropriate some of these big owners' lands, how are we going to have equality? Everyone knows this is what I think. But even some of the reactionary landowners in UNAG voted for me for president. People know what the meaning of my struggle is. I'm not fighting to be rich myself. Everyone knows that. It's for equality and it has always been. I'm struggling for peace but not peace with hunger.

"We don't put any fault, really, on the people who want an individual parcel and who are duped by the reactionaries. You know, we have lived a long time under this system of every man for himself. It's hard to change. We know that."

"Now I won't have to watch my children die . . ."

During our conversation with Asunción, the others gathered around us. At this point, we turned to another member of the cooperative, a middle aged woman, Amanda Espinoza. How has the revolution changed your life? we asked.

"Eleven of my children have died—six at birth and five at less than one year. I have eight who are living. Now I won't have to watch my children die anymore.

"Now we have land we can work. My children have better health because we are eating better. See all the food in these sacks you are sitting on and what we can show you in the storage room. This is an example for those who don't want to work in a cooperative. Many times before we only ate two times a day because we didn't have enough. Before we used to eat meat once a month—now twice a week.

"And my children won't be destroyed by disease. We can take them to the health clinic in Tola."

What is missing now? What would you say that you need now that you don't have? Amanda thought before she spoke.

"A cow to give us milk for the children."

Laundry hanging out to dry in San Carlos

A Priest in Nicaragua

Our trip was coming to an end. The next morning we would have to be at the airport at 5 A.M. for the flight to Miami. Exhausted, we decided to spend our last afternoon in Nicaragua on the beach at San Juan del Sur. The water was magnificent in the late afternoon sun. There were no other tourists.

Joining us for fish and beer in a funky, open air cafe near the beach were Peter Marchetti, the American Jesuit who was our guide for much of the trip, and the Swiss and Canadian workers with their sons. Our conversation was animated and light-hearted. But before we left to go home, we wanted to hear more from Peter, our invaluable guide.

Our conversation then turned to the role of *La*

Peter Marchetti

Prensa, the country's virulently anti-revolution newspaper. Peter told us of his own experience with *La Prensa's* journalistic standards.

"Each morning I celebrate Mass with a congregation that tends to be rich and against the revolution. *La Prensa* published an article about me, saying that all the faithful had left the congregation, that I was driving them out by being openly supportive of the government. They said people just got up and walked out during the Mass. *La Prensa* went front page on just hearsay. That would constitute grounds for libel in most countries.

"Do you know what this was based on? On *three* people leaving before the Mass was over! So I called each of these people to see why they left. Well, one left to go to the bathroom, one left to go to the beach and one left to go call *La Prensa!*"

Needless to say, we laughed pretty hard. Unfortunately, the issue is deadly serious. *La Prensa* is convincing many people that the Sandinistas and government supporters are alienating the Church.

We wanted to know more about how Peter sees his own role in Nicaragua, both as a priest and also as a supporter of the revolution through his work in the Ministry of Agricultural Development.

"Well," Peter told us, "we Jesuits in Nicaragua have questioned a number of things the government has done—like shutting down *La Prensa* from time to time, jailing some communists and a few businessmen for breaking national security laws, and relocating 10,000 Miskito Indians. But we continue to support the government. Now to my father—a bit of an anarchist who taught me from my earliest days a lack of faith in big government—this is an "iffy" proposition. The state is a greedy animal, he always told me.

"But we Jesuits are taking the risk. We're putting our name behind this imperfect reality. We do so for only one reason—because the government continues to respond to the needs of the poor. As long as it does that, it will have our support.

"The Church has implicitly supported many governments who have not cared in the least for God's poor. So my brethren in Nicaragua and El Salvador see no reason for withdrawing our support from one that does and—who knows—one that may be able to offer to the world a third way, distinct from that of capitalism and socialism as we know it."

"Nicaragua is a school"

On the plane back to Miami we were quiet, absorbing the many impressions we had gathered in Nicaragua. Above all, we found ourselves asking: Can a small, poor country in the "backyard" of the United States build a society based on meeting the needs of the vast majority of its people—poor, hungry, illiterate? And can it, at the same time, create a democracy in which everyone's voice is heard?

In our journey through Nicaragua, we were struck again and again by the clarity of vision and determination of the Nicaraguans. We were impressed by the flexibility and pragmatism of the leadership. And we came to understand how many Nicaraguans are moved by their Christian faith to align themselves with the poor majority.

We came to see the Sandinistas not as rigid ideologues who lift their policies from Marxist manifestos but as reasonable people who admit their mistakes and try to learn from them. "Nicaragua is a school" is how they often explained the evolution of their policies in light of their experiences.

We were impressed by how many Nicaraguans are vitally engaged in building their new society. From Jesús, who scrambled us eggs from the new egg cooperative, to David, who talked about his work with the CDS neighborhood committee, all across the country Nicaraguans are working to change their lives.

Arriving in the Miami airport our musings stopped. We picked up the *Miami Herald* and the *Wall Street Journal* and were rudely reminded that our government sees a very different Nicaragua than the one we had just seen.

We were reminded that our government seems unwilling to view the complex reality of Nicaragua today through the eyes of Nicaraguans—like so many of those we met. For them, the revolution appears as their first real hope ever. Instead, the United States government can see Nicaraguans only as "puppets of the expansionist Soviet Union," a threat to our security.

What Does Our Government Fear?

Discovering that four decades of support for the Somozas could not prevent the Sandinista-led government from taking power, the U.S. government under President Carter initially tried to find a *modus vivendi* with the Sandinistas. By contrast, President Reagan came in swinging. The 1980 Republican platform called for "rolling back" the Nicaraguan revolution.

The Reagan administration's belligerence has been unrelenting. Overcoming the legacy of underdevelopment, rebuilding from the ruins of war, recovering from the devastating 1982 floods—all are made even more difficult by the U.S. government's campaign of threats, covert interventions, and arming of Nicaragua's hostile neighbors.

Apparently feeling threatened by the new Nicaraguan government's priorities, President Reagan authorized a $19 million CIA plan to finance paramilitary units to blow up bridges and power stations. His administration cut off U.S. aid to the Nicaraguan government and pressured other governments to follow suit. In defiance of U.S. law, the administration has turned a blind eye to paramilitary camps in Florida where ex-Somoza Guardsmen train for counterrevolution. At the World Bank, where the United States wields a quarter of the voting power, it lobbied against Nicaragua; at the Inter-American Development Bank it blocked a proposed $30 million loan to help rebuild Nicaragua's commercial fishing fleet—which would have provided both jobs and cheap protein for Nicaraguan workers.

The Reagan administration has also tripled military aid to neighboring Honduras and encouraged its army to harass Nicaragua.

Calling Nicaragua a "Marxist-Leninist" state, the Reagan administration chooses to ignore the fact that after three years of revolution the bulk of both industry and agriculture remain in private hands.

Calling Nicaragua a major human rights violator, the Reagan administration chooses to ignore on-site investigations by a variety of human rights organizations. Amnesty International, Americas Watch, and Pax Christi International, as well as the Organization of American States, have all concluded that there's a world of difference for the better between Nicaragua today and Nicaragua under the Somoza dictatorship.

Calling Nicaragua "totalitarian," the Reagan administration chooses to ignore the considerable freedoms—of speech, of religion, of association and of the press—certainly greater than found in most other Latin American countries supported by the United States.

The Reagan administration could have chosen to encourage the changes in justice, in civil liberties and in food, farming, health and education which have improved the lives of the majority of Nicaraguans since victory over the Somoza dictatorship:

—The new government has more than tripled

expenditures for health and education, compared to even the best year under Somoza.

—The infant death rate has been reduced by one-third. This measure is universally recognized as the most telling indicator of family nutrition and the availability of health services.

—Almost 40,000 landless rural families have received access to land where they can grow food.

—Production of basic foods is up—corn by 10 percent, beans by 45 percent, and rice by 100 percent compared to 1977-78.

—Consumption of basic foods has soared—corn by a third, beans by 40 percent and rice by 30 percent since 1978.

—A volunteer-based literacy campaign dramatically cut the illiteracy rate from over half of the population to less than one-seventh. Over 1,200 new schools have been constructed, nearly all in the countryside.

These advances reflect the government's pledge to ground its priorities in what it calls the "logic of the majority." Ignoring these advances, our government chooses to increase its belligerence, exaggerating Nicaragua's shortcomings to the point of distortion. Yet nothing we have learned about Nicaragua—during Joe's ten visits and the journey we made together or from piles of documents and interviews in Washington—indicates Nicaragua is a threat to the people of the United States.

So why do Reagan administration officials feel so threatened? we wonder.

What if Nicaragua *does* develop differently from so many other revolutions? What if the budding elements of democracy we have identified—from the grassroots organizations to the Council of State—do flower? And what if at the same time the Nicaraguan revolution succeeds in meeting the basic needs of the poor majority for food, housing, and health care? What if the Sandinistas help to teach us all that there *could* be more than two models of development, that it *is* possible to make profound structural changes which allow for both democratic participation and justice?

Perhaps the U.S. government realizes that the potential threat of Nicaragua is not military or economic: it is the threat of a good example which could inspire the majority in so many countries throughout the world who still suffer impoverishment and tyranny similar to that under Somoza. It is the threat of a good example, an example desperately awaited from El Salvador to the Philippines to Poland.

Perhaps the U.S. government fears that if the Nicaraguan revolution were allowed to flower it might make it that much harder to defeat revolutionary movements of the poor and hungry throughout the world.

If it's the threat of a good example that is behind our government's hostility toward Nicaragua, then there is another, more sobering lesson for Americans: We may never know whether a vision like that of the Sandinistas can be realized as long as we maintain in power in Washington those intent on denying it even a chance.

Nicaragua Resource Guide

Books

1. Aleman, Luis; Cendales, Lola; Marino, German; McFadden, John; Peresson, Mario; Suarez, Maria; Tamez, Carlos; *Vencimos: La Cruzada Nacional de Alfabetización* de Nicaragua: Libro Abierto Para America Latina, International Development Research Centre, Box 8500, Ottawa, Ontario, Canada K1G 3H9. Definitive work on the Nicaraguan literacy campaign written by participants in the effort. In Spanish only.

2. Bevan, John and Black, George, *The Loss of Fear: Education in Nicaragua Before and After the Revolution.* From National Solidarity Campaign, 20 Compton Terrace, London N1.

3. Black, George, *Triumph of the People—The Sandinista Revolution in Nicaragua,* Zed Press

(London). Excellent and thorough resource. $7.95 plus $1.50 postage from National Network in Solidarity with the Nicaraguan People (NNSNP), 930 - "F" Street NW #720, Washington, DC 20004, (202) 223-2328 or (202) 628-9598.

4. Cardenal, Ernesto, *The Gospel in Solentiname,* Orbis Books (Maryknoll, New York), 1976.

5. Cardenal, Ernesto, *Zero Hour and Other Documentary Poems,* New Direction Books (New York), 1980.

6. Collins, Joseph, with Frances Moore Lappé and Nick Allen, *What Difference Can a Revolution Make? Food and Farming in the New Nicaragua,* Institute for Food and Development Policy (San Francisco), 1982. Sympathetic yet critical report on food and farming policies of new Nicaraguan government. $4.95 from IFDP, 1885 Mission Street, San Francisco, CA 94103.

7. EPICA Task Force, *Nicaragua: A People's Revolution.* 100-page primer. $4.25 plus $.75 postage from EPICA, 1470 Irving Street NW, Washington, DC 20010.

8. Hinde, Peter, *Look! A New Thing in the Americas.* A Carmelite priest looks at the role of the church in Nicaragua. $1.00, available in bulk from National Network.

9. Meiselas, Susan, *Nicaragua June '78-July '79,* Pantheon Books (New York), 1981. Color photo-

graphs and chronology. $11.95.

10. Millet, Richard, *Guardians of the Dynasty: A History of the U.S.-Created Guardia National de Nicaragua and the Somoza Family*, Orbis Books (Maryknoll, New York), 1977.

11. Randall, Margaret, *Sandino's Daughters*, New Star Books (Vancouver and Toronto), 1981. From the Crossing Press, Trumansberg, NY 14886.

12. Selser, Gregorio, *Sandino*, Monthly Review Press (New York), 1981.

13. Walker, Thomas, *Nicaragua in Revolution: An Anthology*, Praeger (New York), 1981.

14. Weber, Henri, *Nicaragua: The Sandinist Revolution*, New Left Review Editions (London), 1981.

15. Wheelock, Jaime, *Imperialismo y Dictadura*, Siglo XXI (Mexico City), 3rd edition, 1979.

Articles and Pamphlets

1. Cardenal, Fernando and Miller, Valerie, "Nicaragua 1980: The Battle of the ABC's," *Harvard Educational Review*, vol. 50, no. 1, February 1981, pp. 1-19. Reprint $1 from 13 Appian Way, Cambridge, MA 02138.

2. Council on Interracial Books for Children, "The Literacy Crusade in Nicaragua," *Interracial Books for Children*, vol. 12, no. 2, 1981. Reprint $1 from National Network.

3. Landis, Fred, "CIA Psychological Warfare Operations: How the CIA Manipulates the Media in Nicaragua, Chile, and Jamaica," *Science for the People*, vol. 14, no. 1, Jan/Feb 1982. Available from Science for the People, 897 Main Street, Cambridge, MA 02139.

4. "New Fact Sheets on Nicaragua." Fact sheets on Destabilization, Government and Mass Politics, Women, Atlantic Coast, Agrarian Reform, and Church. $7 per packet from National Network.

5. North American Committee on Latin America, *Target Nicaragua*. Special January-February 1982 issue on destabilization, counterrevolution, the Atlantic Coast, and U.S. maneuvers in the region. $3.75 postpaid from NACLA, 151 West 19th Street, 9th Floor, New York, NY 10011.

6. Trueman, Beverly, "Nicaragua's Second Revolution" and "1984: 'The Revolution is Not a Piata,'" *Christianity and Crisis*, vol. 41, no. 17, Nov. 2, 1981. $1 from Christianity and Crisis, 537 West 121st Street, New York, NY 10027.

Periodicals

1. *Envio*, monthly "letter" on political, economic, and social developments in Nicaragua from the

Jesuit-run Instituto Historico de Centroamerica. Very useful. Available in English, Spanish, or German. $25 per year from Apartådo A©194, Managua, Nicaragua.

2. *NACLA Report on the Americas*, bimonthly, NACLA, 151 West 19th Street, New York, NY 10011. $15 per year.

3. *Nicaragua*, bimonthly, National Network, address above. $5.00 per year, U.S.; $8.00, Mexico/ Canada; $10.00 elsewhere.

4. *Nicaragua Update*, bimonthly, Nicaragua Interfaith Committee for Action (NICA), 942 Market Street, Room 709, San Francisco, CA 94102, (415) 433-6057. $7.00.

5. *Nicaraguan Perspectives*, quarterly, Nicaragua Information Center, P. O. Box 1004, Berkeley, CA 94704, (415) 549-1387. $10 per year.

6. *WOLA Update*, bimonthly plus special reports, Washington Office on Latin America, 110 Maryland Avenue NE, Washington, DC 20002. $10.00 per year.

Films

1. *From the Ashes*, 16mm, color, 60 min, English subtitles, available from Document Associates, 211 E. 43rd Street, New York, NY 10017, (212) 682-0730. The reconstruction of Nicaragua from the point of view of one family.

2. *Sandino Hoy y Siempre*, 16mm, color, 57 min, English subtitles, available from Icarus Films, 200 Park Avenue South, Suite 1319, New York, NY 10003. A portrait of Nicaragua and its people during the reconstruction process.

3. *Sandino Vive!*, 16mm, color, 28 min, 1980, Spanish or English, free loan from Maryknoll, Maryknoll, NY. The church's role in the overthrow of Somoza.

4. *Thanks to God and the Revolution*, 16mm, color, 30 min, English subtitles, available from Icarus Films. An inquiry into the role of Christians in social change and armed struggle.

5. *These Same Hands (Nicaragua: Las Mismas Manos)*, ¾-inch videocassette format, 53 min, available from World Focus Films, 2125 Russell Street, Berkeley, CA 94705, (415) 848-8126. $50 rental, $250 purchase (no 16mm version).

6. *The Uprising*, 35mm, color, 96 min, Spanish or English, available from Kino International, 250 West 57th Street, New York, NY 10019, (212) 586-8720. Director Peter Lilienthal's dramatization of events during the final period of fighting in 1979.

7. *Women in Arms*, 16mm, color, 59 min, Spanish or English, available from Hudson River Productions, P. O. Box 515, Franklin Lakes, NJ 07417. Par-

ticipation of women in the war and the transformation of society.

Tape and Slide Shows

1. "Central America: Roots of the Crisis," 27 min, 131 slides, available from American Friends Service Committee, Latin American Program, 1501 Cherry Street, Philadelphia, PA 19102, (215) 241-7159. $50 purchase, $15 one-week rental. (Revised and updated, August 1981.) A look at the history, economics, and politics of the current situation in the region.

2. "Nicaragua: The Challenge of Revolution," 25 min, 139 slides/tape presentation with script and information packet, available from National Network, $15.00 rental. Describes the most important developments in the revolutionary process.

3. "Nicaragua Libre," 20 min, 80 b/w slides, available from Jeanne Gallo, SND, 24 Curtis Avenue, Somerville, MA 02144, $65 purchase. Social conditions and history of struggle plus the effort to build a new society.

4. "Now We're Awakened! Women in Nicaragua," 30 min, 80 color slides/tape and information packet, $15 rental from National Network, $75 purchase from PAN, 410 Merritt #7, Oakland, CA 94610. Women's participation in the overthrow of the dictatorship and the building of a new order in Nicaragua.

Organizations

1. National Network in Solidarity with the Nicaraguan People (NNSNP), 930 - "F" Street NW, #720, Washington, DC 20004, (202) 223-2328 or (202) 628-9598.

2. Nicaragua Interfaith Committee for Action (NICA), 942 Market Street, Room 709, San Francisco, CA 94102, (415) 433-6057.

3. North American Congress on Latin America (NACLA), 151 West 19th Street, New York, NY 10011.

4. Washington Office on Latin America (WOLA), 110 Maryland Avenue NE, Washington, DC 20002.

5. Institute for Food and Development Policy (IFDP), 1885 Mission Street, San Francisco, CA 94103, (415) 864-8555.

Institute Publications

What Difference Could a Revolution Make? Food and Farming in the New Nicaragua, provides a critical yet sympathetic look at the agrarian reform in Nicaragua since the 1979 revolution and analyzes the new government's successes, problems, and prospects. Joseph Collins and Frances Moore Lappé, with Nick Allen, 160 pages. $4.95

Diet for a Small Planet: Tenth Anniversary Edition, an updated edition of the bestseller that taught Americans the social and personal significance of a new way of eating. Frances Moore Lappé, 432 pages with charts, tables, resource guide, recipes, Ballantine Books. $3.50

Development Debacle: The World Bank in the Philippines, uses the World Bank's own secret documents to show how it ambitious development plans actually hurt the very people they were supposed to aid—the poor majority. Walden Bello, David Kinley, and Elaine Elinson, 270 pages with bibliography and tables. $6.95

Food First Comic, a comic for young people based on the book *Food First: Beyond the Myth of Scarcity*. Leonard Rifas, 24 pages. $1.00

Trading the Future: How Booming Farm Exports Threaten Our Food Security traces the worldwide shift from food self-sufficiency to export dependence and shows how U.S. grain exports accelerate this trend. James Wessel, with Frances Moore Lappé and Mort Hantman, 150 pages. $4.95 (est.)

Seeds of the Earth: A Private of Public Resource? examines the rapid erosion of the earth's gene pool of seed varieties and the control of the seed industry by multinational corporations. Pat Roy Mooney, 126 pages with tables and corporate profiles. $7.00

World Hunger: Ten Myths clears the way for each of us to work in appropriate ways to end needless hunger. Frances Moore Lappé and Joseph Collins, revised and updated, 72 pages with photographs. $2.95

El Hambre en el Mundo: Diez Mitos, a Spanish-language version of *World Hunger: Ten Myths* plus additional information about food and agriculture policies in Mexico, 72 pages. $1.45

Food First: Beyond the Myth of Scarcity, 50 questions and responses about the causes and proposed remedies for world hunger. Frances Moore Lappé and Joseph Collins, with Cary Fowler, 620 pages, Ballantine Books, revised 1979. $3.95

Aid as Obstacle: Twenty Questions about our Foreign Aid and the Hungry demonstrates that foreign aid may be hurting the very people we want to help and explains why foreign aid programs fail. Frances Moore Lappé, Joseph Collins, David Kinley, 192 pages with photographs. $4.95

Needless Hunger: Voices from a Bangladesh Village exposes the often brutal political and economic roots of needless hunger. Betsy Hartmann and James Boyce, 72 pages with photographs. $3.50

What Can We Do? An action guide on food, land and hunger issues. Interviews with over one dozen North Americans involved in many aspects of these issues. William Valentine and Frances Moore Lappé, 60 pages with photographs. $2.95

Mozambique and Tanzania: Asking the Big Questions looks at the questions which face people working to build economic and political systems based on equity, participation, and cooperation. Frances Moore Lappé and Adele Beccar-Varela, 126 pages with photographs. $4.75

Circle of Poison documents a scandal of global proportions, the export of dangerous pesticides to Third World countries. David Weir and Mark Schapiro, 101 pages with photos and tables. $3.95

Casting New Molds: First Steps towards Worker Control in a Mozambique Steel Factory, a personal account of the day-to-day struggle of Mozambique workers by Peter Sketchley, with Frances Moore Lappé, 64 pages. $3.95

Agrarian Reform and Counter-Reform in Chile, a firsthand look at some of the current economic policies in Chile and their effect on the rural majority. Joseph Collins, 24 pages with photographs. $1.45

Research Reports. "Land Reform: It Is the Answer?

A Venezuelan Peasant Speaks." Frances Moore
Lappé and Hannes Lorenzen, 17 pages. *$1.50*
"Export Agriculture: An Energy Drain." Mort Hant-
man, 50 pages. *$3.00*

Seeds of Revolution is a provocative documentary
about hunger, land reform, multinational agribusi-
ness, and the military in Honduras. Produced by
Howard Enders for ABC News, with the assistance of
joseph Collins, 30 minutes, 16 mm color. *$450* pur-
chase, *$50* rental

Food First Slideshow/Filmstrip in a visually positive and powerful portrayal demonstrates that the
cause of hunger is not scarcity but the increasing
concentration of control over food producing resources, 30 minutes. *$89* (slideshow), *$34* (filmstrip)

Write for our free publications catalogue.
All publications orders must be prepaid.

Institute for Food and Development Policy
1885 Mission Street
San Francisco CA 94103 USA
(415) 864-8555

About the Institute

The Institute for Food and Development Policy, publisher of this book, is a not-for-profit public education center. Founded in 1975 by Frances Moore Lappé and Joseph Collins, the Institute focuses on food and agriculture, always asking: Why hunger in a world of plenty?

By working to identify the root causes of hunger and food problems here and abroad, the Institute provides countermessages:

— No country in the world is a hopeless basket case.

— The illusion of scarcity is a product of the unequal control over food-producing resources; inequality in control over these resources results in their underuse and misuse.

— The hungry are not our enemies. Rather, we and they are victims of the same economic forces which are undercutting their food security as well as ours.

Financial Support

The Institute solicits contributions from individuals, church groups, and private foundations. More and more, it depends on individual contributions, the sale of Institute publications, and speaking honoraria.

We are especially grateful to have the continuing support of the many Institute Sustainers and Friends of the Institute.

In addition to this broad base of international support, we want to thank current foundation and individual supporters. (Financial support does not necessarily reflect agreement with the views expressed in Institute publications.)

Friends of the Institute

Because the Institute's work threatens many established interests, we believe that our effectiveness depends on developing the widest possible base of support. By joining the Friends of the Institute program you can receive our expanding list of publications at a generous discount of free, while contributing in a fundamental way to the ongoing work of the Institute.

All contributors of $25 or more receive a free copy of the paperback edition of the highly acclaimed *Food First: Beyond the Myth of Scarcity* by Frances Moore Lappé and Joseph Collins with Cary Fowler (Ballantine, 1979). Contributors of $100 or more also receive one free copy of all major Institute publications for one year. Contributors of $25 or more also receive a 50 percent discount on one copy of all Institute publications for one year.

All contributions are tax-deductible.

Dear Institute,

( ) *Yes, I support the kind of work you are doing—such as this book on Nicaragua. I'd like to become a Friend of the Institute.*

( ) *Please send me more information about the Institute, including your publications catalog.*

(Mail to IFDP, 1885 Mission St., San Francisco, CA 94103 USA.)

Name _____

Address _____

City/State/Zip/Country _____

Telephone _____

What Difference Could a Revolution Make?

reports on the dramatic changes in food and farming brought about by the first three years of the Sandinista revolution. How have the lives of the rural poor and the rural rich changed? Are the hungry eating better? How has food production—both for local consumption and for export—been affected? This book comes up with some surprising answers.

In telling the story of the new government's efforts to build a food and farming system that can meet the needs of the country's poor majority, while increasing production of export crops to earn foreign exchange, it shatters the myths about Nicaragua created in Washington.

What Difference Could a Revolution Make? documents how the Sandinista agrarian reform is pragmatic and non-doctrinaire, innovative and production-oriented.

$4.95

Food and Farming in The New Nicaragua

by Joseph Collins
with Frances Moore Lappé and Nick Allen